Succeed on the Standardized Test

This Book Includes:

- 2 Performance Based Assessments (PBA)
- 2 End-Of-Year (EOY) Assessments
- Detailed Answer explanations for every question
- Type I questions - Concepts, Skills and Procedures
  Type II questions - Expressing Mathematical Reasoning
  Type III questions - Modeling and/or Applications
- Strategies for building speed and accuracy
- Content aligned with the new Common Core State Standards

Plus access to Online Workbooks which include:

- Hundreds of practice questions
- Self-paced learning and personalized score reports
- Instant feedback after completion of the workbook

Complement Classroom Learning All Year

Using the Lumos Study Program, parents and teachers can reinforce the classroom learning experience for children. It creates a collaborative learning platform for students, teachers and parents.

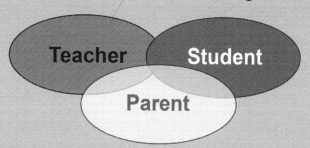

Used in Schools and Public Libraries
To Improve Student Achievement

Lumos Learning

Common Core Assessments and Online Workbooks: Grade 7 Mathematics, PARCC Edition

Contributing Editor   - **Aaron Spencer**
Contributing Editor   - **Gregory Applegate**
Contributing Editor   - **Nikki McGee**
Curriculum Director   - **Marisa Adams**
Executive Producer   - **Mukunda Krishnaswamy**
Designer and Illustrator - **Harini Nagaraj**

ISBN-10: 1940484227

ISBN-13: 978-1-940484-22-8

Printed in the United States of America

For permissions and additional information contact us

Lumos Information Services, LLC
PO Box 1575, Piscataway, NJ 08855-1575
http://www.LumosLearning.com

Email: support@lumoslearning.com
Tel: (732) 384-0146
Fax: (866) 283-6471

Lumos Learning

Table of Contents

Introduction   **1**
How to use this book effectively   2
PARCC Frequently Asked Questions   3
How to access the Lumos Online Workbooks   5
Lumos StepUp™ Mobile App FAQ   6
Lumos SchoolUp™ Mobile App FAQ   7
Test Taking Tips   8

Performance Based Assessment (PBA) - 1   **9**
Performance Based Assessment (PBA) - 1 Answer Key   16
Performance Based Assessment (PBA) - 1 Detailed Explanations   17

Performance Based Assessment (PBA) - 2   **22**
Performance Based Assessment (PBA) - 2 Answer Key   30
Performance Based Assessment (PBA) - 2 Detailed Explanations   32

End-Of-Year Assessment (EOY) - 1   **37**
End-Of-Year Assessment (EOY) - 1 Answer Key   49
End-Of-Year Assessment (EOY) - 1 Detailed Explanations   51

End-Of-Year Assessment (EOY) - 2   **60**
End-Of-Year Assessment (EOY) - 2 Answer Key   70
End-Of-Year Assessment (EOY) - 2 Detailed Explanations   72

Introduction

The Common Core State Standards Initiative (CCSS) was created from the need to have more robust and rigorous guidelines, which could be standardized from state to state. These guidelines create a learning environment where students will be able to graduate high school with all skills necessary to be active and successful members of society, whether they take a role in the workforce or in some sort of post-secondary education.

Once the CCSS were fully developed and implemented, it became necessary to devise a way to ensure they were assessed appropriately. To this end, states adopting the CCSS have joined one of two consortia, either PARCC or Smarter Balanced.

What is PARCC?

The Partnership for Assessment of Readiness for College and Careers (PARCC) is one of the two state consortiums responsible for developing assessments aligned to the new, more rigorous Common Core State Standards. A combination of educational leaders from PARCC Governing and Participating states, along with test developers, have worked together to create the new computer based English Language Arts and Math Assessments.

PARCC has spent the better part of two years developing their new assessments, and in many ways, they will be unlike anything many students have ever seen. The tests will be conducted online, requiring students to complete tasks to assess a deeper understanding of the CCSS. Additionally, instead of one final test at the end of the year, PARCC understands that the best way to measure student success is to assess them multiple times a year. So, students in PARCC states will take a mid-year assessment called a Performance Based Assessment (PBA) and an End-of-Year Assessment (EOY).

How Can the Lumos Study Program Prepare Students for PARCC Tests?

Beginning in the fall of 2014, student mastery of Common Core State Standards will be assessed using standardized testing methods. At Lumos Learning, we believe that year-long learning and adequate practice before the actual test are the keys to success on these standardized tests. We have designed the Lumos study program to help students get plenty of realistic practice before the test and to promote year long collaborative learning.

This is a Lumos **tedBook**™. It connects you to Online Workbooks and additional resources using a number of devices including Android phones, iPhones, tablets and personal computers. The Lumos StepUp Online Workbooks are designed to promote year-long learning. It is a simple program students can securely access using a computer or device with internet access. It consists of hundreds of grade appropriate questions, aligned to the new Common Core State Standards. Students will get instant feedback and can review their answers anytime. Each student's answers and progress can be reviewed by parents and educators to reinforce the learning experience.

 LumosLearning.com

How to use this book effectively

The Lumos Program is a flexible learning tool. It can be adapted to suit a student's skill level and the time available to practice before standardized tests. Here are some tips to help you use this book and the online workbooks effectively:

Students
- Take one Performance Based Assessment (PBA).
- Use the "Related Lumos StepUp™ Online Workbook" in the Answer Key section to identify the topic that is related to each question.
- Use the Online workbooks to practice your areas of difficulty and complement classroom learning.
- Download the Lumos StepUp™ app using the instructions provided in Lumos StepUp™ Mobile App FAQ to have anywhere access to online resources.
- Have open-ended questions evaluated by a teacher or parent, keeping in mind the scoring rubrics.
- Take the second PBA as you get close to the test date.
- Complete the test in a quiet place, following the test guidelines. Practice tests provide you an opportunity to improve your test-taking skills and to review topics included in the PARCC test.
- As the end of the year becomes closer, take one EOY and follow the above guidelines before taking the second.

Parents
- Familiarize yourself with the PARCC test format and expectations.
- Help your child use Lumos StepUp™ Online Workbooks by following the instructions in "How to access the Lumos Online Workbooks" section of this chapter.
- Download the Lumos SchoolUp™ app using the instructions provided in the Lumos SchoolUp™ Mobile App FAQ section of this chapter to get useful school information.
- Review your child's performance in the "Lumos Online Workbooks" periodically. You can do this by simply asking your child to log into the system online and select the subject area you wish to review.
- Review your child's work in the practice PBA's and EOY's.

Teachers
- Please contact **support@lumoslearning.com** to request a **teacher account.** A teacher account will help you create custom assessments and lessons as well as review the online work of your students. Visit **http://www.lumoslearning.com/math-quill** to learn more.
- Download the Lumos SchoolUp™ app using the instructions provided in Lumos SchoolUp™ Mobile App FAQ to get convenient access to Common Core State Standards and additional school related resources.
- If your school has purchased the school edition of this book, please use this book as the Teacher Guide.
- You can use the Lumos online programs along with this book to complement and extend your classroom instruction.

PARCC Frequently Asked Questions

What Will PARCC Math Assessment Look Like?

For Math, PARCC differentiates three different types of questions:

Type I – Tasks assessing concepts, skills, procedures (Machine scorable only)
- Balance of conceptual understanding, fluency, and application
- Can involve any or all mathematical practice standards
- Machine scorable including innovative, computer-based formats
- Will appear on the End of Year and Performance Based Assessment components

Type II - Tasks assessing expressing mathematical reasoning
- Each task calls for written arguments/justifications, critique of reasoning or precision in mathematical statements (MP.3, 6).
- Can involve other mathematical practice standards
- May include a mix of machine-scored and hand-scored responses
- Included on the Performance Based Assessment component

Type III - Tasks assessing modeling/applications
- Each task calls for modeling/application in a real-world context or scenario (MP.4)
- Can involve other mathematical practice standards
- May include a mix of machine-scored and hand-scored responses
- Included on the Performance Based Assessment component

The PBA will be administered once 75% of the school year is complete. It will consist of Type I, Type II, and Type III questions. In the PBA, students will be given a set amount of time to complete their tasks.

The time for each PBA is described below:

Estimated Time on Task in Minutes (PBA)		
Grade	Session One	Session Two
3	50	50
4	50	50
5	50	50
6	50	50
7	50	50
8	50	50

LumosLearning.com

The EOY will be administered once 90% of the school year is complete. It will consist of Type I questions only. In the EOY, students will also be given a set amount of time to complete their tasks.

The time for each EOY is described below:

Estimated Time on Task in Minutes (EOY)		
Grade	Session One	Session Two
3	55	55
4	55	55
5	55	55
6	55	55
7	55	55
8	55	55

What is a PARCC Aligned Test Practice Book?

Inside this book, you will find four full-length practice tests that are similar to the standardized tests students will take to assess their mastery of CCSS-aligned curriculum. Completing these tests will help students master the different areas that are included in newly aligned standardized tests and practice test taking skills. The results will help the students and educators get insights into students' strengths and weaknesses in specific content areas. These insights could be used to help students strengthen their skills in difficult topics and to improve speed and accuracy while taking the test.

How is this Lumos tedBook aligned to PARCC Guidelines?

Although the PARCC assessments will be conducted online, the practice tests here have been created to accurately reflect the depth and rigor of PARCC tasks in a pencil and paper format. Students will still be exposed to the Technology Enhanced Constructed-Response (TECR) style questions so they become familiar with the wording and how to think through these types of tasks.

This edition of the practice test book was created in the Summer 2014 and aligned to the most current PARCC standards released to date. Some changes will occur as PARCC continues to release new information in the fall of 2014 and beyond.

Where can I get more information about PARCC?

You can obtain up-to-date information on PARCC, including sample assessment items, schedules, & the answers to frequently asked questions from the PARCC website at **http://www.parcconline.org**

Where can I get additional information about the Common Core State Standards (CCSS)?

Please visit **http://www.corestandards.org/Math**

How to access the Lumos Online Workbooks

First Time Access:

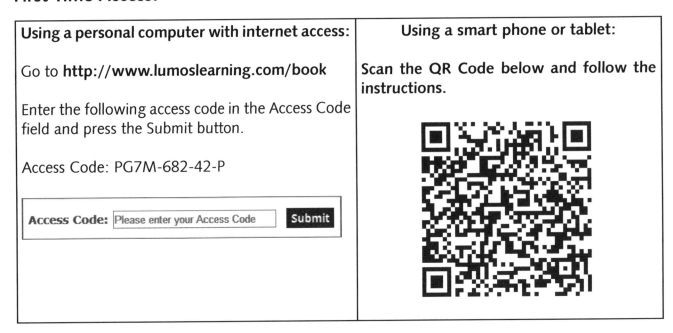

Using a personal computer with internet access:	Using a smart phone or tablet:
Go to **http://www.lumoslearning.com/book**	Scan the QR Code below and follow the instructions.

For the computer: Enter the following access code in the Access Code field and press the Submit button.

Access Code: PG7M-682-42-P

In the next screen, click on the "New User" button to register your user name and password.

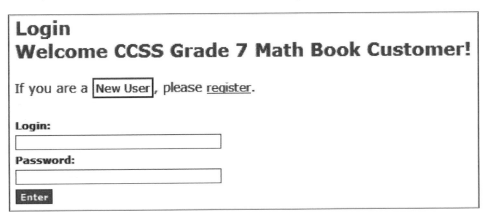

Login
Welcome CCSS Grade 7 Math Book Customer!

If you are a [New User], please register.

Login:

Password:

[Enter]

Subsequent Access:

After you establish your user id and password for subsequent access, simply login with your account information.

What if I buy more than one Lumos Study Program?
Please note that you can use all Online Workbooks with one User ID and Password. If you buy more than one book, you will access them with the same account.

Go back to the **http://www.lumoslearning.com/book** link and enter the access code provided in the second book. In the next screen simply login using your previously created account.

LumosLearning.com

Lumos StepUp™ Mobile App FAQ For Students

What is the Lumos StepUp™ App?

It is a FREE application you can download onto your Android smart phones, tablets, iPhones, and iPads.

What are the Benefits of the StepUp™ App?

This mobile application gives convenient access to Common Core State Standards, Practice Tests, Online Workbooks, and learning resources through your smart phone and tablet computers.

Do I Need the StepUp™ App to Access Online Workbooks?

No, you can access Lumos StepUp™ Online Workbooks through a personal computer. The StepUp™ app simply enhances your learning experience and allows you to conveniently access StepUp™ Online Workbooks and additional resources through your smart phone or tablet.

How can I Download the App?

Visit **lumoslearning.com/a/stepup-app** using your smart phone or tablet and follow the instructions to download the app.

**QR Code
for Smart Phone
Or Tablet Users**

Lumos SchoolUp™ Mobile App FAQ For Parents

What is the Lumos SchoolUp™ App?

It is a FREE App that helps parents and teachers get a wide range of useful information about their school. It can be downloaded onto smartphones and tablets from popular App Stores.

What are the Benefits of the Lumos SchoolUp™ App?

It provides convenient access to
* School performance reports.
* School "Stickies". A Sticky could be information about an upcoming test, homework, extra curricular activities and other school events. Parents and educators can easily create their own sticky and share with the school community.
* Common Core State Standards.
* Sample questions.
* Educational blogs.
* StepUp™ student activity reports.

How can I Download the App?

Visit **lumoslearning.com/a/schoolup-app** using your smartphone or tablet and follow the instructions provided to download the App. Alternatively, scan the QR Code provided below using your smartphone or tablet computer.

QR Code
for Smart Phone
Or Tablet Users

Is SchoolUp™ available for Apple Devices?

SchoolUp™ will be available for Apple devices in the future. The initial release is supported on the Android platform. However, users with iPhones or iPads can use the web version of SchoolUp™ by logging on to **lumoslearning.com/a/schoolup**

       LumosLearning.com

Test Taking Tips

1) **The day before the test, make sure you get a good night's sleep.**

2) **On the day of the test, be sure to eat a good hearty breakfast! Also, be sure to arrive at school on time.**

3) **During the test:**

- **Read every question carefully.**

    - Do not spend too much time on any one question. Work steadily through all questions in the section.
    - Attempt all of the questions even if you are not sure of some answers.
    - If you run into a difficult question, eliminate as many choices as you can and then pick the best one from the remaining choices. Intelligent guessing will help you increase your score.
    - Also, mark the question so that if you have extra time, you can return to it after you reach the end of the section. Try to erase the marks after you complete the work.
    - Some questions may refer to a graph, chart, or other kind of picture. Carefully review the graphic before answering the question.
    - Be sure to include explanations for your written responses and show all work.

- **While Answering Multiple-Choice (EBSR) questions.**

    - Completely fill in the bubble corresponding to your answer choice.
    - Read all of the answer choices, even if think you have found the correct answer.

- **While Answering TECR questions.**

    - Read the directions of each question. Some might ask you to drag something, others to select, and still others to highlight. Follow all instructions of the question (or questions if it is in multiple parts)

Performance Based Assessment (PBA) - 1

Student Name:
Test Date:

Start Time:
End Time:

Here are some reminders for when you are taking the Grade 7 Mathematics Performance Based Assessment (PBA).

To answer the questions on the test, use the directions given in the question. If you do not know the answer to a question, skip it and go on to the next question. If time permits, you may return to questions in this session only. Do your best to answer every question.

---

1. Kelsey wants to compare the number of blouses that she owns of various colors. She owns a total of 30 blouses. 20% of them are blue. Five of them are red. $\frac{3}{10}$ of them are white. The rest are either pink, purple, or green. What simplified fraction would correctly represent the portion of the blouses that are either pink, purple, or green? Write your answer in the box below.

$\frac{?}{5}$ of the blouses are pink, purple, or green.

2. Which numerical value would represent the probability of an event that is neither highly likely to occur nor highly unlikely to occur, and why?

   Ⓐ 0.53, because this number is not very close to 0 (highly unlikely) nor very close to 1 (highly likely).

   Ⓑ 0.91, because this number represents a probability that is not impossible to take place (a probability of 0), but is not certain, either (a probability of 1).

   Ⓒ 13, because this represents a probability that is not impossible (0) but still has a chance of taking place.

   Ⓓ 47, because a number that is about halfway between 0 and 100 represents a probability that is about halfway between impossibility and certainty.

    LumosLearning.com   ▲

3. Which expression would be equivalent to: $\dfrac{1+b}{2} - 3(a-1)$

    Ⓐ   2b - 3a + 5

    Ⓑ $\dfrac{b - 6a}{2} + 4$

    Ⓒ   2b - 3a + $\dfrac{7}{2}$

    Ⓓ $\dfrac{b - 6a + 7}{2}$

4. A number of friends went on fishing trips this summer. Each stayed a certain number of days and caught a certain number of fish during their trip. According to the table, whose ratio of fish caught per day is proportional to Brian's?

Fishing Trip					
	Brian	Kevin	Justin	Brody	York
Days	3	4	2	5	4
Fish Caught	21	25	12	35	20

    Ⓐ Kevin

    Ⓑ Justin

    Ⓒ Brody

    Ⓓ York

5. Aaron wants to plant an orchard of apple trees. Based upon what he has studied, he can expect that 90% of the trees he plants will survive the first year. Of those that survive the first year, he can expect that 95% will survive permanently. If he is going to plant 300 trees this spring and another 500 the following spring, how many trees should he expect to have in his orchard permanently? Write your answer in the box below.

    _____ Trees

6. At the grocery store, Kim's pre-tax total cost is $58.75. Sale's tax is added at a rate of 4.75%. However, for this weekend only, her state is allowing the purchase of all school supplies tax-free. 20% of what Kim is purchasing is school supplies. What will her total cost be after tax is added? Round to the nearest cent. Write your answer in the box below.

    Total cost after tax: $ _____

7. Jim and Rose love to play dominoes together. They have a double-twelve set of dominoes that contains 91 dominoes. Jim is going to build a nice custom storage box for them. His dominoes are professional size: 2 in x 1 in x 3/8 in. He is going to build the box in the shape of a rectangle that is 4.2 in x 6.2 in. How deep does the box need to be at minimum if it is going to be able to hold all 91 dominoes? Write your answer in the box below.

The box must be at least [ ] in deep.

8. Jessica and Lindsey are curious as to who owns the most pairs of shoes. Jessica counts her shoes and finds that she owns 18 pairs of shoes. When Lindsey counts hers, she finds that she owns only approximately 72% as many pairs of shoes as Jessica. How many pairs of shoes does she own? Write your answer in the box below.

[ ] pairs of shoes.

9. Keith has a small summer business taking care of people's lawns in his neighborhood. He finds that working by himself, he has to work about 27 hours each week to take care of all his clients' needs. If he hires his brother to help him, together they are able to work about 50% faster together than Keith was able to work alone. How many hours will they have to work each week in order to get the same amount of work done? Write your answer in the box below.

[ ] Number of hours each week

10. Leo's family is going to buy a new television. An electronics store is advertising a big sale in which all televisions are 10% off the regular price. In addition to this, Leo's father has a special coupon that allows him to take $200 off the price of any one item with a regular price over $1,000. The $200 discount will be taken after the 10% discount. Assuming that the television Leo's dad is going to purchase does have a regular price over $1,000, which of the following is NOT a correct expression of the price that Leo's dad will have to pay for a television that has a regular price of p dollars?

Ⓐ 0.90p – 200

Ⓑ (p – 200) – 0.10p

Ⓒ (p – 200)(0.90)

Ⓓ p(1 – 0.10) – 200

11. Jason is building a new addition to his house. It is a rectangular room that is 15 feet x 12 feet in dimensions. One of the 15-foot walls of the room will be part of the existing house. He is trying to calculate how many 8-foot long two by fours (2 inch by 4 inch boards) he needs to purchase for the framing of the new room. He knows that he has to place a two by four stud in the wall every 16 in. He cannot leave a space larger than that without a two by four. At each of the new corners of the room (not the existing ones), he will use three two by fours for reinforcement. At the corners where the room connects to the existing portion of the house, only one stud will be needed. In the box below, give a written explanation how Jason can go about calculating the number of two by fours he should purchase. How many will he need?

PART A

Number of two by fours needed. Write your answer in the box below:

```
┌─────────────────────┐
│                     │
│                     │
└─────────────────────┘
```

PART B

How do you know? Write your explanation in the box below:

```
┌──────────────────────────────────────────────────────────────────┐
│                                                                    │
│                                                                    │
│                                                                    │
│                                                                    │
│                                                                    │
│                                                                    │
└──────────────────────────────────────────────────────────────────┘
```

12. Jamie thought he had correctly solved the equation that was on the board, but his answer was not the correct one. Here is his work. Explain what Jamie did wrong and what he needed to do differently to solve the equation correctly:

$$\frac{2(a-5)+6a+3}{4} = 4.25$$

$$\frac{2a-10+6a+3}{4} = 4.25$$

$$\frac{8a-7}{4} = 4.25$$

$$2a - 7 = 4.25$$

$$2a = 11.25$$

$$a = 5.625$$

Write your explanation in the box below.

```



```

13. Callie wants to create a scenario using the roll of a six-sided die. She wants the scenario only to allow the die roller to be successful about 40 times out of 120 people who will attempt it. She wants to require that the roll of the die result in a number higher than a certain value. Explain to her what number she should require the third roll to be higher than and why.

PART A

The third roll should be higher than a _____. Write your answer in the box below.

```


```

PART B

How do you know? Write your explanation in the box below.

```



```

14. Annabelle wants to make curtains for two windows in her living room. The windows are each 3 ft wide. The material that she has is just the right size to match the height of the windows. The material she has is in a 9 foot roll, to be used for both windows together. She decides that she wants the curtains to be wide enough to extend a little bit beyond the window on each side. If she uses the whole roll of material, explain how she can calculate how far the curtains will be able to extend on each side of the windows and give the distance they will extend.

PART A

The distance the curtains will extend is _____. Write your answer in the box below.

```


```

LumosLearning.com   ▲

PART B

How do you know? Write your explanation in the box below.

```


```

15. A sports equipment manufacturing company currently sells a certain tennis racket for $20.00. It costs them $11.50 to produce it.

    PART A

    Write a formula that represents the profit P the company makes on this racket based upon the number n of rackets they sell.

    ```

    ```

    PART B

    Adapt the formula to show how the profit changes based upon a production cost increase of a dollars. Explain how your formula correctly reflects the cost change.

    ```

    ```

16. Gary is balancing his checking account with his spending. His checking account shows a balance of $750.83. He has accounted for all of the deposits and purchases he has made except for one transaction. He cannot remember the exact cost of a pen set he purchased as a gift for a number of friends. He also can not remember exactly how many of the sets he purchased. Not including that purchase, he has calculated that his account balance should be $855.83. Using rational numbers for n and p, write an expression in the form of: Balance + (n)(–p) to represent one possible scenario for the number of pen sets purchased, n, and the price of each set, p. Explain why this form of the expression makes sense and why the numbers you have chosen for n and p make sense in this scenario. Write your answer in the box below.

17. Haley is starting a small business that provides catered lunches to business at their offices on a weekly basis. She already has 5 weekly clients and has reasonable expectations of finding 2 more each month. Each client pays her $200 weekly for her services.

PART A

Write an equation that would represent the gross income Haley can expect on a weekly basis in a certain amount of months if m=months. Write your equation in the box below.

PART B

Explain how you created your equation. Write your answer in the box below.

End of Performance Based Assessment (PBA) - 1

     LumosLearning.com   ▲

Performance Based Assessment (PBA) - 1

Answer Key

Question No.	Answer	Related Lumos Online Workbook	CCSS
1	$\frac{1}{3}$	Solving Real World Problems	7.NS.3
2	A	Understanding Probability	7.SP.5
3	D	Rational Numbers, Multiplication & Division	7.NS.2c
4	C	Understanding and Representing Proportions	7.RP.2a
5	684	Solving Multi-Step Problems	7.EE.3
6	$60.98	Solving Real World Problems	7.NS.3
7	3	Finding Area, Volume, & Surface Area	7.G.6
8	13	Applying Ratios and Percents	7.RP.3
9	18	Understanding and Representing Proportions	7.RP.2c
10	C	Interpreting the Meanings of Expressions	7.EE.2
11 Part A & B	34	Rational Numbers, Multiplication & Division	7.NS.2b-2
12	*	Solving Multi-Step Problems	7.EE.3
13 Part A & B	Higher than a 4	Using Probability Models	7.SP.7a
14 Part A & B	9 inched on either side	Solving Multi-Step Problems	7.EE.3
15 Part A	8.50n	Modeling Using Equations or Inequalities	7.EE.4
15 Part B	(8.50 – a)n	Modeling Using Equations or Inequalities	7.EE.4
16	855.83 + (5) (-21.00)	Rational Numbers, Addition & Subtraction	7.NS.1c-1
17 Part A & B	I = (5 + 2m)(200)	Modeling Using Equations or Inequalities	7.EE.4a-1

* See detailed explanation

Performance Based Assessment (PBA) - 1

Detailed Explanations

Question No.	Answer	Detailed Explanation
1	$\dfrac{1}{3}$	If 20% of the blouses are blue, that is the same as one fifth of them, or 6 altogether. Five are red. 3 out of 10 are white, which means that 9 of them are white. Altogether, that makes a total of 20 blouses accounted for, leaving 10 for the remaining category. The fraction would be $\dfrac{10}{30}$ which simplified to $\dfrac{1}{3}$
2	A	The range of probability when expressed as a decimal is 0 to 1. Anything close to 0 is unlikely; anything close to 1 is likely; 0.53 is near the middle and thus is neither highly likely nor highly unlikely.
3	D	If we distribute the expression, get a common denominator, and write the whole thing as one fraction, we will have the answer, D: $$\frac{1+b}{2}-3(a-1)=$$ $$\frac{1+b}{2}-3a+3=$$ $$\frac{1+b}{2}+\frac{-6a+6}{2}=$$ $$\frac{b-6a+7}{2}$$
4	C	Brian's ratio is 3:21, which simplifies to 1:7. Brody's ratio is 5:35, which also simplifies to 1:7. They are proportional.
5	684	Consider all the trees together, which gives a total of 800. If 90% survive the first year, that makes (800)(0.90) = 720 trees. If 95% of those survive permanently, that makes (720)(0.95) = 684 trees.
6	$60.98	To calculate the tax, we must take only 80% of the total cost of the items and multiply it by the tax rate of 4.75%: (58.75)(0.80)(0.0475) = $2.23 Add this to the pre-tax price: $58.75 + $2.23 = $60.98

LumosLearning.com   ▲

Question No.	Answer	Detailed Explanation
7	3	The dimensions of the box allow for dominoes to be stored in the shape of four rows one direction and three rows another. This allows for 12 dominoes per level, then. How many levels will have to be stacked on top of one another? Simply divide: $91 \div 12 = 7.58$. The box will need to be able to hold 8 levels. Multiply by the thickness of the dominoes: $(8)(3/8) = 3$ inches.
8	13	Multiply the 18 pairs of shoes that Jessica owns by 72%: $(18)(0.72) = 12.96$. Because the percentage given to us was approximate, we can safely assume that Lindsey owns 13 pairs of shoes.
9	18	Because they are able to work 50% faster, this means that they accomplish 150% as much, or 1.5 times as much. Divide the number of hours by 1.5: $(27) \div 1.5 = 18$ hours.
10	C	The problem with answer C is that the $200 discount is being taken before the 10% discount. Looking at the mathematical expression, you can see that the 0.90 will be distributed to the price of the television and the $200 discount. The result is that the discount becomes only 90% of $200.
11 Part A & B	34	Each wall must be considered separately. A 12 ft wall has a total of 144 inches. Starting on the end connected to the existing house, how many studs will be needed? Dividing the distance by 16 in, we have exactly eight 16 in distances. We must start with a stud at the corner that is connected to the existing portion of the house, and then we must place eight more studs, one after each of the 16 in distances, giving a total of 9 studs. At the corner, however, there will be three studs (one is already counted in the 8), as the details said, so we must count two more. This means that the 12 ft wall, plus the corner, needs a total of eleven studs. The same is true for each of the 12 ft walls, for a total of twenty-two studs between them. Now we must count the number of studs needed in the 15 ft wall. The corners are already accounted for by the other walls. We must simply have enough studs between the corners. 15 ft is a total of 180 in. Dividing by 16 in, we have 11.25. We will need twelve studs, then, between the corners. Altogether, then, we need a total of thirty-four studs.

Question No.	Answer	Detailed Explanation
12		Jamie did everything well until near the end of the process. When he divided by 4, he only divided the 8a and did not distribute the division to the 7 as he needed to do. The correct work would look like this: $$\frac{2(a-5)+6a+3}{4} = 4.25$$ $$\frac{2a-10+6a+3}{4} = 4.25$$ $$\frac{8a-7}{4} = 4.25$$ $$2a - 1.75 = 4.25$$ $$2a = 6$$ $$a = 3$$
13 Part A & B	Higher than a 4	Basically, Callie wants the success rate of the roll of the die to be 40 out of 120, which simplifies to 1 out of 3. Because there are 6 numbers on the die that might be rolled, a proportional success rate would mean 2 of the 6 numbers should work. Thus, if the roll must be higher than 4, that means that either 5 or 6 (two numbers out of the six) will work. This will match Callie's desired success rate.
14 Part A & B	9 inches on either side	The roll of material is a total of 9 feet. Dividing by 2 in order to give an equal amount of material to each window, we see that each window will have 4.5 feet available to it. If 3 feet of material is needed to cover the window, that leaves 1.5 feet, or 18 inches, of extra length. Half of that must be on each side of the window, which means that there will be 9 inches of overlap on each side.
15 Part A	$P = 8.50n$	Because each racket sells for $8.50 more than the production cost, this is the amount of profit per racket. Multiplying by the number of rackets sold, we will have the total profit.
15 Part B	$P = (8.50 - a)n$	If the cost of production increases, the profit per racket decreases by that same amount. Thus, we have to subtract a dollars from the previous 8.50 profit per racket before multiplying by the number of rackets sold.

LumosLearning.com ▲

Question No.	Answer	Detailed Explanation
16	855.83 + (5) (-21.00)	We see that a negative change of $105 is to be accounted for by the purchase of the pen sets. One possible way that this might take place is if Gary purchased 5 sets at $21.00 each. In such a case, we would add (5)(–21.00), noting that the price of each set should be negative in order to show that these funds are being taken out of our account for the purchase.
17 Part A & B	I = (5+2m) (200)	The number of clients is currently 5. That is projected to increase by 2 each month, giving a total of 5 + 2m. That number must then be multiplied by 200 per client in order to find out the total gross income that can be expected.

Notes

 LumosLearning.com

Performance Based Assessment (PBA) - 2

Student Name:
Test Date:

Start Time:
End Time:

Here are some reminders for when you are taking the Grade 7 Mathematics Performance Based Assessment (PBA).

To answer the questions on the test, use the directions given in the question. If you do not know the answer to a question, skip it and go on to the next question. If time permits, you may return to questions in this session only. Do your best to answer every question.

1. **What value of B would make this statement true:** $\frac{B}{3}(2 + BC) = 12C + 4$

   Ⓐ 4

   Ⓑ 2

   Ⓒ 6

   Ⓓ 9

2. Micah is a busy college student. He carries a full load of classes and works a full time job to support himself financially while in college. Last semester, his total number of hours between job and classes each week usually amounted to about 80 hours. He has decided that he cannot do so many hours each week this semester. He feels that he has to cut back to about 80% as many hours. If half of his hours are to be school hours, how many school hours will he spend each week this semester? Write your answer in the box below.

   School hours this semester

3. Patrick is working for his uncle doing some construction work on a house his uncle is building. His uncle owes him $800 already for the work he has done, but is going to pay him $250 per week. In the meantime, Patrick is still going to work a bit more for him each week. His uncle is going to owe him an extra $100 each week for the additional work that he is going to be doing. Which of the following expressions correctly represents how much his uncle will owe him after t weeks?

    Ⓐ 800 – 350t

    Ⓑ 700 – 250t

    Ⓒ 900 – 250t

    Ⓓ 800 – 150t

4. In order to win the board game he is playing, Taylor needs two things to happen. First, he is going to roll a six-sided die and needs to roll number greater than 2. Second, he has to draw a card from a deck of numbered cards. The deck contains cards with the numbers 1-20 on them. There is one card with each number. He needs to draw a number that is a multiple of 4. What is the probability that he is going to win the game? Express your answer in the form of a simplified fraction and write it in the box below.

    [_____] Probability

5. Using the diagram with the given angle measures, find the value of c.

    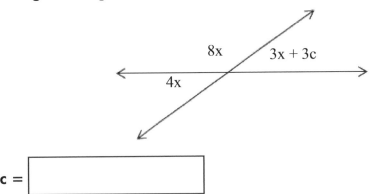

    c = [_____]

6. Jake has been asked to mow his grandparents' yard. It is a large yard at 1.2 acres. He is trying to figure out how much time it will take him to mow their yard. He knows that his parents' rectangular yard is about 40 yards x 24 yards and takes him about 1 hour to mow. He also knows there are 4,840 square yards in an acre.

       ▼

PART A

How long will it take Jake to mow his grandparents' yard? Write the answer in the box below.

_____

PART B

How did you determine your answer? Write your explanation in the box below.

7. Greg is building an outbuilding from concrete blocks. The building is going to be a 25 ft x 35 ft rectangle. The block walls will be 10 ft tall. The concrete blocks he is using have a face that is 16 in by 8 in. He has already laid two rows of block all the way around the perimeter of the building. He is able to lay an average of 30 blocks per hour. To the nearest tenth of an hour, how many more hours will it take him to lay the rest of the blocks for the building? Do not account for door or window spaces or overlapping of blocks in the corner areas.

_____ Hours Remaining.

8. In a representational survey, 20% of voters were questioned as to which candidate they voted for.

PART A

If 328 of the voters in the survey voted for Jerry Smith, how many votes must he have received altogether if the survey was accurate. Write your answer in the box below.

_____

PART B

How did you determine your answer? Write your explanation in the box below.

$$\begin{array}{|c|}\hline \\ \\ \\ \\ \\ \\ \hline \end{array}$$

9. In a shop class, Allen is going to build a scale model of a rectangular house. If the full scale house would have a square footage of 1,800 square feet, how many square inches will Allen's scale model be if he builds it on a linear scale of 1:36? Write your answer in the box below.

$$\boxed{} \; in^2$$

10. Simplify the complex fraction. Assume all factors are non-zeroes:

$$\dfrac{\left(\dfrac{6(a+b)(b-a)}{(ab+3)(2a+ab)}\right)}{\left(\dfrac{(3b-3a)}{(b+2)(a^2b+3a)}\right)}$$

Write your answer in the box below. Do not write your answer in factored form.

Simplified expression: $\boxed{}$

11. A clothing company has designed a matching outfit of a pair of slacks and a shirt to go with it. The two items can be purchased together as a set or separately. They predict that 60% of buyers will buy the set together, 30% will buy only the shirt, and 10% will buy only the slacks. They have decided that they are going to produce 9,000 of the shirts. They are trying to decide how many pairs of the slacks they should produce in order best to meet the proportional demand for each item.

PART A

How many they should produce. Write your answer in the box below.

$$\boxed{} \; \text{Number of pairs of slacks to produce.}$$

PART B

How can they calculate that number correctly? Explain how you determined your answer in the box below.

[ ]

12. The Birch family wants to save some money on their utility bill by hanging some of their clothes outside on a line to dry rather than using their dryer to do so. They know that they cannot dry all their clothes on the line because of the lack of space and time, so they plan to use the dryer for only two drying loads per week. Their washing machine holds an extra-large capacity that is 1.5 times as much as their dryer will hold. Their clothes line holds only half as much clothing as their dryer does.

PART A

If they have to wash enough clothes each week to fill their washing machine 4 times, how many times will they have to fill the clothes line in order to dry their clothes each week? Write your answer in the box below.

[ ]

PART B

Explain the process of how you can find the correct answer.

[ ]

13. Leslie wants to build a 1,200 piece jigsaw puzzle. The completed puzzle will be in the shape of a rectangle that is 40 pieces in length by 30 pieces in width. Each piece is a square with an area of 0.25 in².

PART A

If Leslie wants to build the puzzle on a table that is at least 6 inches larger on all four sides than the complete puzzle, so that it makes a 6 inch border around the puzzle, what are the minimum dimensions of the table that she will need?

PART B

Explain how to calculate this. Write your explanation in the box below.

14. Polly and Joan are working on some review problems for math class. They have x hours to do as many problems today as they can. These problems will each take approximately 10 minutes. They want to figure out approximately how many problems they can expect to complete today. When they each do the calculations, however, they arrive at different answers. The starting expressions for each Polly and Joan are shown below.

PART A

Which of them set the problem up correctly?

Ⓐ Polly: Number of problems $= \dfrac{x}{0.10}$

Ⓑ Joan: Number of problems $= \dfrac{x}{\left(\dfrac{1}{6}\right)}$

PART B

Explain how you know and what was wrong with one of the expressions in the box below.

15. The population of Philip's hometown is on the rise. One way of expressing the population each year is by taking the previous year's population and considering the changes based on all citizens who have left and all who have newly arrived.

If P_n represents the new population, P_o the old population, N the newly arrived citizens and L the citizens who have left, give an equation that combines these together in a way that will correctly calculate the new population.

PART A

Express the new population only in terms of a sum of these terms and not a difference of the terms.

PART B

Explain your equation.

16. Timothy has begun selling copies of his first work of art. In the first year, he sold 200 copies. In the second year, he sold 240 copies. In the sixth year, he sold 400 copies. Suppose that he continues to increase his sales at the same rate.

PART A

Write an equation that will help Timothy calculate how many copies of his work he can expect to sell each year after y years.

PART B

Explain how you arrived at this equation.

```
[                                                        ]
[                                                        ]
[                                                        ]
[                                                        ]
[                                                        ]
```

PART C

Suppose that Timothy sells the copies of his work for $25.00. During what year will he be able to make an income of $21,000 from sales. Write your answer in the box below

```
[                    ]
[                    ]
```

17. Tisha started a petition for lawmakers to change a certain law. As word spreads, more and more people are showing interest. She is gaining about 500 signatures each week.

PART A

If 2,000 people signed the petition initially, write an equation that will show the number of signatures that can be expected each week after w weeks. Write your answer in the box below.

```
[                    ]
[                    ]
```

PART B

Suppose that the amount of time that it took to get 500 new signatures decreased from 1 week to 5 days. Explain how this would affect your equation. Write the explanation in the box below.

```
[                                                        ]
[                                                        ]
[                                                        ]
[                                                        ]
[                                                        ]
```

End of Performance Based Assessment (PBA) - 2

▼

Performance Based Assessment (PBA) - 2

Answer Key

Question No.	Answer	Related Lumos Online Workbook	CCSS
1	C	Applying Properties to Rational Expressions	7.EE.1
2	32	Solving Real World Problems	7.NS.3
3	D	Modeling Using Equations or Inequalities	7.EE.4
4	$\frac{1}{6}$	Finding the Probability of a Compound Event	7.SP.8a
5	5	Angles	7.G.5
6 Part A	6 hours and 3 minutes	Finding Area, Volume, & Surface Area	7.G.6
6 Part B	*	Finding Area, Volume, & Surface Area	7.G.6
7	39.0	Solving Multi-Step Problems	7.EE.3
8 Part A	1, 640	Sampling a Population	7.SP.1
8 Part B	*	Sampling a Population	7.SP.1
9	200 square inches	Scale Models	7.G.1
10	2a + 2b	Applying Properties to Rational Expressions	7.EE.1
11 Part A	7,000	Understanding and Representing Proportions	7.RP.2c
11 Part B	*	Understanding and Representing Proportions	7.RP.2c
12 Part A	8	Solving Real World Problems	7.NS.3
12 Part B	*	Solving Real World Problems	7.NS.3
13 Part A	32 inches by 27 inches	Modeling Using Equations or Inequalities	7.EE.4a-1
13 Part B	*	Modeling Using Equations or Inequalities	7.EE.4a-1
14 Part A	B	Solving Real World Problems	7.NS.3
14 Part B	*	Solving Real World Problems	7.NS.3

Question No.	Answer	Related Lumos Online Workbook	CCSS
15 Part A	$Pn=Po+N+(-L)$	Rational Numbers, Addition & Subtraction	7.NS.1c-1
15 Part B	*	Rational Numbers, Addition & Subtraction	7.NS.1c-1
16 Part A	$N=200+40(y-1)$	Modeling Using Equations or Inequalities	7.EE.4a-1
16 Part B	*	Modeling Using Equations or Inequalities	7.EE.4a-1
16 Part C	17th year	Modeling Using Equations or Inequalities	7.EE.4a-1
17 Part A	$N=2,000+500w$	Modeling Using Equations or Inequalities	7.EE.4
17 Part B	$\dfrac{7}{5}$	Modeling Using Equations or Inequalities	7.EE.4

Performance Based Assessment (PBA) - 2

Detailed Explanations

Question No.	Answer	Detailed Explanation
1	C	If B = 6, we will have: $$\frac{B}{3}(2+BC)=12C+4$$ $$\frac{6}{3}(2+6C)=12C+4$$ $$2(2+6C)=12C+4$$ $$4+12C=12C+4$$ The expressions are the same value on both sides.
2	32	Multiply the 80% by the previous total of 80 hours per week: (0.80)(80) = 64 hours per week. If half of these are school hours, it will be 32 school hours per week.
3	D	If Patrick receives $250 per week from his uncle, $100 of that will account for the new work he does. That leaves only $150 per week to be applied to the previous wages, which have a starting amount of $800. Thus, we subtract $150 per week from $800.
4	$\frac{1}{6}$	The first event of rolling a number greater than 2 has a probability of $\frac{4}{6}$, which simplifies to $\frac{2}{3}$. For the second event, there are only four cards that are multiples of 4 (4, 8, 12, 16, and 20). This means that five of the twenty cards will work, giving a probability of $\frac{5}{20}$, which simplifies to $\frac{1}{4}$. Multiply the two probabilities together since both events must take place: $$\left(\frac{2}{3}\right)\left(\frac{1}{4}\right)=\frac{2}{12}=\frac{1}{6}$$

Question No.	Answer	Detailed Explanation
5	5	In order to find the value of c, we must first calculate the value of x. The angles with measures of 8x and 4x form a linear pair together, which means their measures must have a sum of 180o: 8x + 4x = 180 12x = 180 x = 15 Now, we also know that the angles with measures of 8x and 3x + 3c form a linear pair, so we can do the same for the measure of those two angles: 8x + 3x + 3c = 180 8(15) + 3(15) + 3c = 180 165 + 3c = 180 3c = 15 c = 5
6 Part A	6 hours and 3 minutes	
6 Part B		Multiply 1. Acres by 4840 to turn it into square yards. Then, calculate the area of his parents' yard in square inches. Set up a proportion with parents' area/1 = grandparents' area/t. Solve the proportion and write your answer in minutes.
7	39.0	The perimeter of the building is a total of 120 ft, or 1,440 in. Each block has a length of 16 inches. Dividing, we see that we need (1,440) ÷ 16 = 90 blocks for one run of blocks around the whole perimeter. This will give 8 in of wall height. We need to reach a total height of 10 ft, or 120 inches. Two rows of blocks have already been laid, which is 16 inches of height. We need an additional 104 inches, so we divide to see how many runs of block we need to add: (104) ÷ 8 = 13 runs. Multiplying by 90 blocks per run, Greg needs to lay (13)(90) = 1,170 blocks. At a rate of 30 blocks per hour, we find that he will need 1,170 ÷ 30 = 39.0 hours.
8 Part A	1, 640	
8 Part B		If 20% of his voters amount to 328 people, we need to multiply by 5 to arrive at how many people would constitute 100% of his voters: (328) (5) = 1,640 voters.

▼

Question No.	Answer	Detailed Explanation
9	200 square inches	The scale given is a linear scale. In order to calculate area, we must multiply two dimensions, length and width. Thus, the scale of the areas will be the linear scale multiplied by itself, which gives us a scale of 1:1,296. Dividing the 1,800 square footage of the house, we have 1.38889 square feet. A square foot is 12 in by 12 in, or 144 square inches, so we multiply by 144: (144)(1.38889) = 200 square inches
10	2a + 2b	The complex fraction must be simplified by multiplying by the reciprocal and cancelling common factors: $$\frac{\left(\dfrac{6(a+b)(b-a)}{(ab+3)(2a+ab)}\right)}{\left(\dfrac{(3b-3a)}{(b+2)(a^2b+3a)}\right)} =$$ $$\left(\frac{6(a+b)(b-a)}{(ab+3)(2a+ab)}\right)\left(\frac{(b+2)(a^2b+3a)}{3b-3a}\right) =$$ $$\left(\frac{6(a+b)(b-a)}{(ab+3)a(2+b)}\right)\left(\frac{(b+2)a(ab+3)}{3(b-a)}\right) =$$ $$2(a+b) =$$ $$2a+2b$$
11 Part A	7,000	
11 Part B		Out of a sample of 10 buyers, 6 will buy both items, 3 more will buy only the shirt, and 1 will buy only the slacks. This gives a total of 9 shirts purchased and 7 slacks, so this should be the ratio we use to determine how many of each item needs to be produced. If the company has decided to manufacture 9,000 shirts, that means they should also produce 7,000 pairs of slacks.
12 Part A	8	
12 Part B		If they are going to wash 4 washing machine loads, that amounts to (4)(1.5) = 6 dryer loads. They are going to use the dryer twice, which leaves 4 dryer loads that must be hung out to dry on the line. Because the line only holds half of a dryer load, this means it will have to be filled 8 times during the week.

Question No.	Answer	Detailed Explanation
13 Part A	32 inches by 27 inches	
13 Part B		If the area of each square piece is 0.25 in, that means that the dimensions must be 0.5 in by 0.5 in. Because the puzzle is 40 pieces by 30 pieces, that gives dimensions of 20 in by 15 in. Adding 6 inches on all four sides of the puzzle, we will have 32 in by 27 in for our minimum table dimensions.
14 Part A	B	Joan's Expression is Correct
14 Part B		Dividing the number of hours available by the amount of time per problem will give us the correct number of problems that can be done in the given time. Converting from minutes to hours, though, is the issue. 10 minutes is not the same as 0.10 hours. 10 minutes is $\frac{10}{60}$ hours, or $\frac{1}{6}$ of an hour.
15 Part A	Pn=Po+N+(−L)	
15 Part B		The key to this expression is to recognize that the sum must be of the opposite of L in order for that number of people to be taken away from the previous year's population.
16 Part A	N=200+40(y−1)	What we see is that each year, the number of copies sold increases by 40. Starting at 200, we will add 40 for each year after the first year. We can express this amount this way.
16 Part B		Income will be the number of copies sold times the price per copy: $I = (25.00)(200 + 40(y - 1))$ Set this equal to 21,000, and solve: $21,000 = (25)(160 + 40y)$ $21,000 = 4,000 + 1,000y$ $17,000 = 1,000y$ $y = 17$ He will make $21,000 in income the 17th year.
16 Part C	17th year	
17 Part A	N=2,000+ 500w	The initial amount is 2,000. We must add 500 more times the number of weeks that have passed.
17 Part B		We now have to calculate how many signatures will be gained each week with the new rate. If 500 signature are gained in only five days, that amounts to 100 signatures per day. Over the span of the seven day week, we can expect to gain 700 signatures. Thus, the new formula will not add 500w, but 700w. The weekly gain is now.

Notes

End-Of-Year Assessment (EOY) - 1

Student Name:

Test Date:

Start Time:

End Time:

Here are some reminders for when you are taking the Grade 7 Mathematics End-of-Year Assessment (EOY).

To answer the questions on the test, use the directions given in the question. If you do not know the answer to a question, skip it and go on to the next question. If time permits, you may return to questions in this session only. Do your best to answer every question.

1.   Greg has just started a new job at a grocery store down the road. He lives within walking distance of it. It takes him 20 minutes to walk there. He lives 2/3 of a mile from the store. Sometimes he rides his bike there instead, and it takes him only half as much time to get there.

PART A

Greg wants to know his speed in MPH when he is walking and when he is riding his bike. Write your answer in the box and give the speed for each in terms of MPH in decimal form to the nearest hundredth.

Speed (in MPH) when walking

Speed (in MPH) when riding his bike

PART B

Sometimes, if Greg is short on time, he has someone drive him to work to save time. The ratio of his travel times when walking compared to riding his bike is proportional to his times when riding his bike compared to driving. Calculate the amount of time in minutes that it takes him when driving.

Time (in minutes) when driving

     LumosLearning.com   ◀

2. Jasmine has opened a bank account with an initial deposit of $200. She has also received a debit card to use for her account. Each week she is able to save $10 to deposit in the account. Her account balance (the amount of money in the account) is her initial deposit of $200 plus any deposits she makes minus any purchases she makes using her debit card.

PART A

Three weeks after Jasmine opened her account, she has made two purchases. She bought a pair of shoes that cost $15.75, and she purchased some music online for a cost of $5.50. Which of the following expressions would correctly represent the amount of money in her account after three weeks:

Ⓐ $200 + $15.75 + $5.50

Ⓑ $200 + (-$15.75) + (-$5.50)

Ⓒ $200 + $15.75 + $5.50 + 3($10)

Ⓓ $200 + (-$15.75) + (-$5.50) +3($10)

PART B

Jasmine's mother has instructed her that she must keep at least the amount of her initial deposit ($200) in the account at all times. Any purchases that she makes must not bring her balance below that amount. After a number of weeks, she has a balance of $225 dollars. She wants to make a purchase of an item that costs $75. Assuming her saving is consistent with the information given above, how many weeks will it be before she is able to purchase the item without dropping below the required $200 balance in her account? Write your answer in the box.

Number of weeks: [   ]

3. The 7th graders in Jennifer's school all take art class as well as math class. The variability (range) of students' grades in art class is about the same as the variability (range) of students' grades in math class. However, the mean of students' grades in math class is significantly lower than that in art class. Which of the following tables of students' grades in each class would represent this situation correctly?

Ⓐ

ART	98	87	93	95	83	42	86	99	91
MATH	87	95	86	45	88	97	96	92	89

Ⓑ

ART	38	95	97	88	80	96	99	85	91
MATH	58	52	77	89	32	75	64	94	78

Ⓒ	ART	55	86	92	87	95	42	53	78	100
	MATH	52	88	87	84	94	96	53	98	97

Ⓓ	ART	86	95	92	87	79	99	100	94	83
	MATH	77	80	73	68	82	55	65	79	99

4. If a circle has a circumference of 32π in, give the area of the circle in terms of π. Write your answer in the box below.

Area: ☐ π in²

5. Which of the following is an equivalent expression to: $-3b[2c + 4 - 5t + (-4c)]$

Ⓐ $-12b + 15bt - 18bc$

Ⓑ $-12b(-2c - 5t)$

Ⓒ $-12b + 15bt - 3b(-2c)$

Ⓓ $-3b(-t - 2c)$

6. The rational number $\frac{3}{5}$ would be an appropriate number to use in considering which of the following scenarios:

Ⓐ There are 50 test questions on an exam. A student wants to know how many he might miss and still miss no more than 30% of the questions.

Ⓑ Mike travelled 50 miles in 30 minutes and wants to calculate his speed in MPH.

Ⓒ Out of 65 students, only 39 of them completed their homework. The teacher wishes to express that as a simplified ratio.

Ⓓ Three friends want to buy a $5 toy together and need to know how much each of them needs to pay.

   LumosLearning.com ◀

7. What shape would be the result of taking a slice from a cube diagonally from the top right edge to the bottom left edge?

    Ⓐ Square
    Ⓑ Rectangle
    Ⓒ Right triangle
    Ⓓ Rhombus

8. Ryan started the summer with 50 chicken eggs in an incubator. Only 84% of the eggs hatched. Of the resulting chicks, 5/6 of them survived the first 3 weeks. If he expects that after 1 year, his number of chickens will be double the number of chicks that survive the first 3 weeks, how many chickens can he expect to have at that time? Write your answer in the box below.

    ┌─────────────────┐
    │   │ chickens.
    └─────────────────┘

9. Timothy has $\frac{2}{5}$ as many games as Grant has for his gaming system. If Grant has 75 games, how many does Timothy have? Write your answer in the box below.

    ┌─────────────────┐
    │   │ games.
    └─────────────────┘

10. Kimberly wants to buy a sweater that is on sale. Assume that A represents the regular price. The sweater is on sale for 20% off the regular price. Which of the following is NOT an accurate representation of the sale price?

    Ⓐ $A - 0.2A$

    Ⓑ $A(0.8)$

    Ⓒ $A(\frac{80}{100})$

    Ⓓ $A(\frac{20}{100})$

11. Which of the following values represents a probability of an event that is likely to happen, and why?

    Ⓐ 0.03, because likely events have a probability close to 0.

    Ⓑ 97.4, because likely events have a probability close to 100%.

    Ⓒ 0.51, because any probability higher than 0.5 is likely to happen.

    Ⓓ 0.95, because likely events have a probability close to 1.

12. In which of the following scenarios would opposite quantities combine to make zero?

- Ⓐ A train travels east 3 miles for 1/3 of an hour.

- Ⓑ Fred works for 30 minutes, and he rests for 30 minutes.

- Ⓒ Kevin earns $24 working for his neighbor and receives a gift of $10 for his birthday, but owes his parents $15 and a friend $18.

- Ⓓ An elevator goes up 3 floors, down 2 floors, up 3 floors, and then down 4 floors.

13. Tommy is 12 years old, and his height is 66 in.

PART A

According to the table below, whose age and height are proportional to Tommy's? Write your answer in the box below.

	Bradley	Savannah	Sarah	Jessica
Age	10	15	6	8
Height (in)	56	69	39	44

's age and height are proportional to Tommy's.

PART B

Explain how you arrived at your answer. Write your explanation in the box below.

LumosLearning.com   ◀

14. Which of the following expressions would be equivalent to the following: $\frac{2}{5}\left(\frac{10}{3}+\frac{25}{6}\right)$

Ⓐ $\left(\frac{2(10)}{8}\right)+\left(\frac{2(25)}{11}\right)$

Ⓑ $\left(\frac{2(10)(25)}{5(3)(6)}\right)$

Ⓒ $\left(\frac{2(10)}{5(3)}\right)+\left(\frac{25}{6}\right)$

Ⓓ $2\left(\frac{2}{3}\right)+\left(\frac{5}{3}\right)$

15. The Greer family is setting their pool up for the summer. The dimensions of their rectangular pool are 15 ft wide x 35 ft long x 9 ft deep. If the hose that they are using to fill the pool puts out water at a rate of 0.84 cubic feet per minute, how long will it take the hose to fill the pool up with water to a level that is 1 foot below the brim of the pool? Write your answer in the box below.

	minutes

16. Lance's mother made a pie last night. Today, there is still half of the pie left. If Lance eats a piece of pie and there is now only $\frac{1}{6}$ of the pie remaining, which of the following is the amount of pie that Lance ate?

Ⓐ $\frac{1}{3}$ of the whole pie

Ⓑ $\frac{1}{4}$ of the whole pie

Ⓒ $\frac{1}{5}$ of the whole pie

Ⓓ $\frac{1}{6}$ of the whole pie

17. The distance travelled by a delivery vehicle can be calculated by the equation Distance = Rate x Time. What would be the correct representation of a situation in which a driver doubles his original speed, but drives for only 1/3 of the original amount of time?

d_n = new distance d_o = original distance

Ⓐ $d_n = 6d_o$

Ⓑ $d_n = \dfrac{3}{2}d_o$

Ⓒ $d_n = \dfrac{2}{3}d_o$

Ⓓ $d_n = \dfrac{1}{6}d_o$

18. The picture shows a corner of a rectangular bedroom. Find the value of c:

Ⓐ 15°
Ⓑ 18°
Ⓒ 90°
Ⓓ 28°

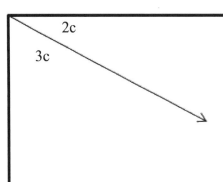

2c

3c

19. Which of the following expressions would be most helpful in multiplying the following without a calculator?: 8(123)

Ⓐ $(4+2+2)(100+10+10+1+1+1)$

Ⓑ $(4)(2)(120+3)$

Ⓒ $(8)(100)+(8)(2)(10)+(8)(3)$

Ⓓ $(4+4)(123)$

20. The following table shows all the possible outcomes that could result from flipping a coin and then rolling a six-sided die:

COIN	H	T	H	T	H	T	H	T	H	T	H	T
DIE	1	1	2	2	3	3	4	4	5	5	6	6

PART A

What is the theoretical probability of flipping a heads and then rolling an even number?

Ⓐ $\dfrac{1}{2}$

Ⓑ $\dfrac{1}{4}$

Ⓒ $\dfrac{5}{12}$

Ⓓ $\dfrac{2}{3}$

PART B

Explain how you determined your answer. Write your explanation in the box below.

21. **PART A**

If the radius of a circle is doubled, by what factor will the area of the circle increase?

Ⓐ The area will also increase by a factor of 2, because the doubled radius is used to calculate the area.

Ⓑ The area will increase by a factor of 4, because the doubled radius is multiplied by 2 when you calculate the area.

Ⓒ The area will increase by a factor of 4, because the factor of 2 by which the radius was increased is then squared when calculating the area.

Ⓓ The area will stay the same, because the doubled radius will then be divided by 2 when calculating the area.

Ⓔ It is impossible to tell by what factor the area will increase unless the actual radius measure is given to us.

PART B

Why? Explain how you determined your answer in the box below.

```



```

22. Use the number line to answer the question:

Which of the following is a correct description of $|P - Q|$

Ⓐ How much greater P is than Q

Ⓑ The distance between P and Q

Ⓒ How much less Q is than P

Ⓓ The opposite of the distance between Q and P.

23. The following table shows how many students are in each grade at a certain high school. In order for a survey of 40 students to be a good basis for drawing conclusions about the general student body of the school, how many 9th graders should be a part of the survey? Write your answer in the box below.

	9th Grade	10th Grade	11th Grade	12th Grade
Number of Students	60	50	50	40

9th grade students should be chosen.

24. x and y are proportional with m and n. If m = 2, n = 7, and x is twice as much as n, what is the value of y?

y = ☐

25. Find the value of A that would make this equation true:

$$6cd + 2b + 9(cd + \frac{b}{3}) = A(3\,cd + b)$$

A = ☐

26. Charlotte is a waitress at a restaurant. The policy at this restaurant is to add an additional 15% tip to every order. If her current customer's order costs a total of $15.75, what is the amount of the tip that she will receive, to the nearest cent? Write your answer in the box below.

Tip: $ ☐

27. Using the scale figure, calculate the area of the square footage of the floor space of the apartment. Write your answer in the box below.

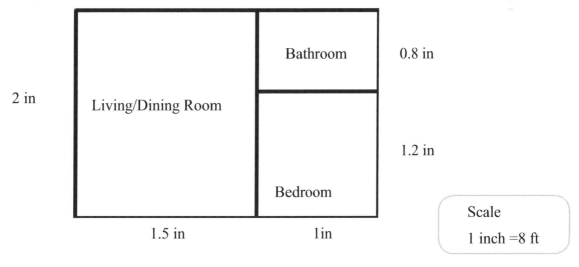

Square footage area: ☐ ft²

28. The lengths and widths of a number of rectangles are given.

Rectangle	A	B	C	D	E	F
Length	10	15	7	30	20	35
Width	14	20	10	42	24	25

PART A

Which other rectangle is proportional in dimensions with rectangle A?

Rectangle [   ] is proportional in dimensions with rectangle A.

PART B

Describe how your determined your answer. Write the explanation in the box below.

29. Scott does not know the amount of the sales tax in the area where he is on vacation. He does recall, however, that he purchased some flip-flops that were on sale recently. The sticker price was $8.00, but they were 25% off. After tax, he ended up paying a total of $6.48. He now wants to buy a beach volleyball set that costs $30.00 before tax. How much will it be after tax? Write your answer in the box below.

Price after tax: $ [   ]

30. Kyle has $75 in saving. He has a summer job that pays him $7.25 per hour. He has to take out about 10% of his earnings for taxes and other expenses, however. How many hours will he have to work before he has at least $500 in savings? Write your answer in the box below.

Number of hours [   ]

LumosLearning.com

31. Which is a simplified version of this complex fraction? Assume that all unknown values are non-zero integers:

$$\frac{\left(\dfrac{2a}{b}\right)}{\left(\dfrac{3c}{5b}\right)}$$

   Ⓐ $\dfrac{5ac}{6b}$

   Ⓑ $\dfrac{6ac}{5b^2}$

   Ⓒ $\dfrac{7ab}{4bc}$

   Ⓓ $\dfrac{10a}{3c}$

32. One circle has an area that is four times as great as that of another circle. How much greater is the radius of the larger circle than that of the smaller circle?

   Ⓐ 4 times as great

   Ⓑ 2 times as great

   Ⓒ 3.14 times as great

   Ⓓ 16 times as great.

33. The ratio of A and B is proportional to the ratio of the square of A and half the square of B. Which of the following correctly describes the relationship between A and B?

   Ⓐ A is the square root of B.

   Ⓑ B is half of A.

   Ⓒ A and B are equal.

   Ⓓ B is twice as much as A.

End of End-Of-Year Assessment (EOY) - 1

End-Of-Year Assessment (EOY) -1
Answer Key

Question No.	Answer	Related Lumos Online Workbook	CCSS
1 Part A	A: Speed when walking: 2 MPH B: Speed when riding his bike: 4 MPH	Unit Rates	7.RP.1
1 Part B	5 minutes	Unit Rates	7.RP.1
2 Part A	D	Modeling Using Equations or Inequalities	7.EE.4
2 Part B	5	Modeling Using Equations or Inequalities	7.EE.4
3	B	Mean, Median, and Mean Absolute Deviation	7.SP.3
4	256π in^2	Circles	7.G.4
5	C	Applying Properties to Rational Expressions	7.EE.1
6	C	Interpreting the Meanings of Expressions	7.EE.2
7	B	Cross Sections of 3-D Figures	7.G.3
8	70 Chickens	Rational Numbers, Multiplication & Division	7.NS.2b-2
9	30 Games	Rational Numbers, Multiplication & Division	7.NS.2
10	D	Interpreting the Meanings of Expressions	7.EE.2
11	D	Understanding Probability	7.SP.5
12	D	Interpreting the Meanings of Expressions	7.EE.2
13 Part A & B	Jessica's age and height are proportional to Tommy's.	Understanding and Representing Proportions	7.RP.2a
14	D	Applying Properties to Rational Expressions	7.EE.1
15	5,000 Minutes	Understanding and Representing Proportions	7.RP.2a

LumosLearning.com ◀

Question No.	Answer	Related Lumos Online Workbook	CCSS
16	A	Rational Numbers, Addition & Subtraction	7.NS.1
17	C	Understanding and Representing Proportions	7.RP.2a
18	B	Angles	7.G.5
19	C	Applying Properties to Rational Expressions	7.EE.1
20 Part A & B	B	Understanding Probability	7.SP.5
21 Part A & B	C	Circles	7.G.4
22	B	Modeling Using Equations or Inequalities	7.EE.4a-1
23	12 9th grade students should be chosen.	Sampling a Population	7.SP.1
24	$y = 49$	Understanding and Representing Proportions	7.RP.2c
25	$A = 5$	Applying Properties to Rational Expression	7.EE.1
26	$2.36	Applying Ratios and Percents	7.RP.3
27	320 ft^2	Scale Models	7.G.1
28 Part A & B	Rectangle D is proportional in dimensions with rectangle A.	Understanding and Representing Proportions	7.RP.2a
29	$32.40	Solving Multi-Step Problems	7.EE.3
30	66 hours	Rational Numbers, Multiplication & Division	7.NS.2b-1
31	D	Applying Properties to Rational Expressions	7.EE.1
32	B	Circles	7.G.4
33	D	Applying Ratios and Percents	7.RP.3-2

End-Of-Year Assessment (EOY) -1

Detailed Explanations

Question No.	Answer	Detailed Explanation
1 Part A	A: Speed when walking: 2 MPH B: Speed when riding his bike: 4 MPH	In calculating the speed, we remember that d = rt. Solving for rate (speed), we have r = d/t. Fill in the distance and time for both walking and riding a bike, converting from minutes to hours in order to have MPH as our units: Walking: $r = \dfrac{2/3}{1/3} = 2MPH$ Biking: $r = \dfrac{2/3}{1/6} = 4MPH$
1 Part B	5 minutes	Set up a proportion of times for walking and biking compared to biking and driving: $\dfrac{20}{10} = \dfrac{10}{x}$ Since 10 is half of 20 on the left side, we know that x must be half of 10 on the right side in order to make it proportional. Thus, the time when driving is 5 minutes.
2 Part A	D	The two purchases are to be subtracted from the initial amount of $200, which is the same thing as adding the opposite values. Also, if three weeks have passed since opening the account, Jasmine has been able to deposit $10 into the account 3 times, which means we add (3)($10).
2 Part B	5	We set up a simple inequality to represent the fact that each week, $10 is added to the current amount of $225, which total must be at least $275 before the purchase can be made: $225 + 10w \geq 275$ Solve: $10w \geq 50$ $w \geq 5$

LumosLearning.com ◀

Question No.	Answer	Detailed Explanation
3	B	To find the range, we must note the least and greatest values in each set of grades. In art class, the lowest grade is 38 and the highest is 99, which gives us a range of 99 – 39 = 60. In math, the lowest grade is 32 and the highest is 94, which gives us a range of 94 – 32 = 62. The ranges are about the same. There is no need to calculate the means exactly, as we can simply note that the other grades in each class are significantly different from one another. The art grades are all in the 80's and 90's, whereas the math grades are in the 50's, 60's, 70's, and only one other in the 80's. The means will be significantly different for each class. In answer options A and C, the ranges are fairly similar, but the grades are much closer together overall, so that the means will not be all that far apart from one another. In answer D, the range for the math class is much larger than the range for grades in the art class.
4	256π in^2	If the circumference is 32π, we can easily find the radius of the circle: $2\pi r = 32\pi$ $r = 16$ With that given radius, we can calculate the area: $A = \pi r^2 = \pi(16)^2 = 256\pi$ in^2
5	C	Starting with our given expression, we simplify: $-3b[2c + 4 - 5t + (-4c)] =$ $-3b[-2c + 4 - 5t] =$ $6bc - 12b + 15bt$ Then, we compare to our answer options, none of which are identical. One of them, however, looks almost the same. We quickly realize that multiplying out the last term of this form gives us 6bc, and now the expressions are identical.
6	C	The fact that 39 out of 65 students completed their homework can be expressed as a ratio of $\dfrac{39}{65}$, which reduces to a simplified form of $\dfrac{3}{5}$.

Question No.	Answer	Detailed Explanation
7	B	In a cube, all of the faces and edges are at right angles. The result will be a quadrilateral with right angles, so it is either a rectangle or a square. The reason that it is not a square is that one dimension of the quadrilateral will be the length of the edge of the cube, while another dimension of the quadrilateral will be the length of the diagonal of one of the square faces of the cube, which must be longer than the edge of the cube.
8	70 Chickens	If 84% of the original 50 chickens hatched, that is a total of 42 chicks: 50(0.84) = 42. If 5/6 of those survive, that leaves us 35: (3/5)(42) = 35. Double that amount, and you have 70 chickens a year later.
9	30 Games	Simply multiply the number of games Grant has, 75, by 2/5: (75) (2/5) = 30 games.
10	D	A ($\frac{20}{100}$) would be the same as saying 20% of the regular price, not 20% off the regular price. All of the other answers amount to a total of 80% of the regular price, which is what the price would be after taking 20% away from the original 100% of the price.
11	D	Because these probabilities are not given in percent form, close to 1 is close to certainty. A probability of 1 is the same as 100% likely. 0.95 is the same as saying 95% probability, which is very likely.
12	D	A total of 6 floors up and 6 floors down would leave the elevator back on the same floor as it started. It is like adding 6 and -6 together to get 0.
13 Part A & B	Jessica's age and height are proportional to Tommy's.	If you divide Tommy's height by his age, you get: $\frac{66}{12} = 5.5$ If you divide Jessica's height by her age, you get: $\frac{44}{8} = 5.5$ The ratio is the same in each case.

    LumosLearning.com

Question No.	Answer	Detailed Explanation
14	D	If you distribute the $\frac{2}{5}$ to both terms within the parentheses, you get: $\frac{2}{5}\left(\frac{10}{3}\right)+\frac{2}{5}\left(\frac{25}{6}\right)$ Simplifying by cancelling common factors, you get: $2\left(\frac{2}{3}\right)+\left(\frac{5}{3}\right)$
15	5,000 Minutes	Because the pool needs to be filled to 1 foot from the brim, we change the height from 9 ft to 8 ft and multiply all three dimensions to find the total volume of water: $15(35)(8) = 4200$ Divide this total volume by the volume of water per minute that the hose puts out and you will have your total time in minutes: $\frac{4200}{0.84} = 5000$ minutes
16	A	$\frac{1}{2}$ of the pie minus how much results in $\frac{1}{6}$ of the pie remaining at the end? $\frac{1}{2}-\frac{1}{3}=\frac{3}{6}-\frac{2}{6}=\frac{1}{6}$ of the pie remaining.
17	C	Consider: $d_o = r_o t_o$ Replace the original rate with twice that amount and the original time with 1/3 that amount, and simplify: $d_n = (2r_o)(\frac{t_o}{3}) = \frac{2}{3}(r_o)(t_o) = \frac{2}{3}d_o$
18	B	Because the room is rectangular, the corner must be a ninety degree angle. Thus, $3c + 2c = 90^o$ $5c = 90^o$ $c = 18^o$

Question No.	Answer	Detailed Explanation
19	C	If you break the number 123 down into its place value parts, you have 100 + 20 + 3. Thus, we can simply multiply 8(100+20+3) and distribute to have: 8(100) + 8(20) + 8(3). The middle term can be simplified even further by rewriting 20 as 10(2). These calculations can easily be done mentally without the aid of a calculator.
20 Part A & B	B	Looking only at the outcomes that start with heads and then end in an even number for the roll of the die, we see that there are a total of 3 possibilities. Altogether, there are 12 total possible outcomes for the two events, so our probability is $\dfrac{3}{12} = \dfrac{1}{4}$.
21 Part A & B	C	Consider the area formula: $A = \pi r^2$. Replace r with 2r to represent a doubling of the radius, and simplify to see what happens: $A = \pi(2r)^2 = \pi(2r)(2r) = 4\pi r^2$. The result is that the area is now 4 times what it was. The reason is not so much that the doubled radius is multiplied by 2. That happens, but incidentally. The reason is that the 2r is all being squared. 2 squared happens to be the same as 2 times 2, but that is coincidental.
22	B	Absolute value is used to describe the distance between two points. The absolute value of a number by itself is its distance from 0. The absolute value of the difference between two points is the distance between them. Because P is to the left of Q on the number line, P – Q will be a negative value. The absolute value signs thus turn that negative into a positive value that represents the distance between the two points without specifying which point is greater.
23	12 9th grade students should be chosen.	Solve: $\dfrac{60}{200} = \dfrac{x}{40}$ $\dfrac{60(40)}{200} = x$ $12 = x$

     LumosLearning.com

Question No.	Answer	Detailed Explanation
24	$y = 49$	Set up a proportion: $$\frac{y}{x} = \frac{n}{m}$$ Fill in the values, recognizing that x must be 14 since it is twice as much as n, which is 7: $$\frac{y}{14} = \frac{7}{2}$$ Solve for y: $$\frac{y}{14} = \frac{7}{2}$$ $$y = \frac{98}{2} = 49$$
25	$A = 5$	Look at the first two terms and factor out the common 2, re-writing it as: $2(3cd + b)$ For the last two terms on that same side, consider: $$9(cd + \frac{b}{3}) = (3)(3)(cd + \frac{b}{3}) = 3(3cd + b)$$ So, rewriting the left side, we have: $2\left(3cd + b\right) + 3\left(3cd + b\right)$, which would be the same thing as 5(3cd + b). Thus, A must be 5.
26	$2.36	Simply take the amount of the bill and multiply by 0.15: $$15.75(0.15) = 2.36$$
27	320 ft²	The easiest way to calculate the square footage of the whole apartment is to find the length and the width of the apartment as a whole and multiply them together. In the scale drawing, the dimensions would be 2 in x 2.5 in. Because the scale says that 1 in is equivalent to 8 ft, we convert the dimensions to 2(8 ft) x 2.5(8 ft), or 16 ft x 20 ft = 320 ft².
28 Part A & B	Rectangle D is proportional in dimensions with rectangle A.	Express the dimensions of rectangle A as a ratio, and simplify: $$\frac{10}{14} = \frac{5}{7}$$ What other rectangle has the same ratio when simplified? Rectangle D: $\frac{30}{42} = \frac{5}{7}$

Question No.	Answer	Detailed Explanation
29	$32.40	If the original price of the flip-flops was $8.00, and they were 25% off, then that brings the price down to $6.00. Thus, the ratio of pre-tax price to after-tax price is $\frac{\$6.00}{\$6.48}$. All items bought under the same sales tax rate will be proportional to this ratio. Thus, we set up a proportion for the $30.00 volleyball set, and solve: $$\frac{\$6.00}{\$6.48} = \frac{\$30.00}{x}$$ $$\frac{\$6.48}{\$6.00} = \frac{x}{\$30.00}$$ $$\$32.40 = x$$
30	66 hours	Set up a simple expression to represent the amount of money Kyle will have. The earnings need to be multiplied by 90% (what is remaining after 10% is taken away) and added to the initial savings of $75: $$75 + (0.90)(7.25h)$$ This expression simplifies when we multiply: $75 + 6.525h$ Then we must set the expression equal to $500, and solve: $$75 + 6.525h = 500$$ $$6.525h = 425$$ $$h \approx 65.13$$ h is a little more than 65 hours, so Kyle must work at least 66 hours to have enough money.
31	D	To simplify this, multiply the top fraction by the reciprocal of the bottom fraction, and simply: $$\frac{\left(\frac{2a}{b}\right)}{\left(\frac{3c}{5b}\right)} = \left(\frac{2a}{b}\right)\left(\frac{5b}{3c}\right) = \frac{10a}{3c}$$
32	B	The ratio of the areas of two circles is always the square of the ratio of the radii. Thus, because we know the ratio of the areas is 1:4, we can take the square root to find the ratio of the radii, giving us a ratio of 1:2. The larger circle has a radius that is twice that of the smaller circle.

LumosLearning.com   ◄

Question No.	Answer	Detailed Explanation
33	D	Set up the proportion according to what you are told:

$$\frac{a}{b} = \frac{a^2}{0.5b^2}$$

What we can do now is to multiply the fraction on the left side of the equation by $\frac{a}{a}$, giving us:

$$\left(\frac{a}{a}\right)\frac{a}{b} = \frac{a^2}{0.5b^2}$$

$$\frac{a^2}{ab} = \frac{a^2}{0.5b^2}$$

We notice that the numerators on each side are now the same, so the denominators must also be the same value as well in order for this equation to be true. We see that if a is the same as 0.5b, then the denominators will be the same. This means that a is half of b, or b is twice the value of a.

Notes

 LumosLearning.com

End-Of-Year Assessment (EOY) - 2

Student Name: **Start Time:**
Test Date: **End Time:**

Here are some reminders for when you are taking the Grade 7 Mathematics End-of-Year Assessment (EOY).

To answer the questions on the test, use the directions given in the question. If you do not know the answer to a question, skip it and go on to the next question. If time permits, you may return to questions in this session only. Do your best to answer every question.

---

1.   A pizza is cut into 8 equal pieces. Jeremy ate 3 of them. Frank ate 2 of them. Then Bill and Harley showed up and shared the rest of the pizza equally. Together, how much of the pizza did Jeremy and Bill eat? Express your answer as a simplified fraction. Write your answer in the box below.

   Jeremy and Bill ate [   ] **of the pizza.**

2.   Mr. Giles is building a set of wooden bunk beds. At one point in the process he is going to take a block of wood and drill a hole from the top of the block straight through the middle of it to the bottom of the block. The drill bit has a circular face. What will be the shape of the hole left in the block of wood where Mr. Giles has drilled?

   Ⓐ   **A cube**

   Ⓑ   **A rectangular prism**

   Ⓒ   **A sphere**

   Ⓓ   **A cylinder**

3.   Anthony has gone on a bike ride that is $3\frac{2}{3}$ miles long. The first part of the ride is almost all uphill. It takes him about 75 minutes to travel   miles. When he reaches the top of the hill, he takes a 10 minute break, turns around, and returns back to where he started along the same path. His total time from start to finish was 1 hour and 55 minutes. What was his average speed in mph while he was returning to where he started? Write your answer in the box below and express the speed in decimal form to two decimal places.

   [   ]

4.   **PART A**

If an event has a probability of 0.93 of taking place, how would you describe the likeliness of that event?

(A)   The event is unlikely. It is a very small number, even below 1.

(B)   The event is neither likely nor unlikely. The value of the probability is in the middle range.

(C)   The event is likely. Any event with a probability that is close to 1 is likely to occur.

PART B

Why? Explain how you determined your answer and write the explanation below.

5.   What is the probability of rolling three even numbers in a row with a six-sided die? Express your answer as a simplified fraction. Write your answer in the box below.

6.   The players on a baseball team are comparing the number of home runs they hit during the season. The third baseman hit twice as many as the second baseman. The first baseman's and shortstop's numbers are proportional with those of the third baseman and second baseman. If the second baseman hit 4 homeruns more than the shortstop, how many more homeruns did the 3rd baseman hit than the 1st baseman? Write your answer in the box below.

⎿_____⎤ more homeruns

7. Samantha has found a great deal on an acoustic guitar, but she doesn't have enough money saved up to buy it. She convinces her parents to loan her $150 so that she can buy it. At the end of each week that Samantha has not paid back the loan, she has to add $3 to how much she owes her parents. If she is able to save up enough money to pay her parents back $20 each week, which of the following expressions correctly represents how much she will still owe her parents after t weeks?

    Ⓐ   150 + 23t

    Ⓑ   153 – 20t

    Ⓒ   150 + 20t – 3t

    Ⓓ   150 – 17t

    Ⓔ   130 – 3t

8. A circle with a radius of $2x + 4$ has an area of 100 ft². What is the area of a circle with a radius of $3x + 6$? Write your answer in the box below.

    □ ft²

9. The Smiths are cattle farmers. They currently have 100 mature head of cattle. As a general rule, they expect 9 out of every 10 calves to survive each year. They normally have about 6 calves to every 10 mature head of cattle in a given year. This year they are going to sell half of the calves that survive. The rest they will keep to increase their herd size. How many total head of cattle will be in their herd after they sell half the calves? Write your answer in the box below.

    □ total head of cattle.

10. Which of the following scenarios includes a number and its additive inverse?

    Ⓐ   Jan sells her MP3 player to her friend for the same amount that she owes her friend

    Ⓑ   Pat buys 100 golf balls for $10

    Ⓒ   A circle's diameter is twice its radius

    Ⓓ   York plays 3 tennis matches in one third of a year

11. Farmer Bill is preparing his fields for planting. As he cultivates them using his equipment, a big factor in how long it takes is how dry or wet the fields are from rain. Assuming a rain fall of 1 inch of rain, consider the following: If it has rained in the last 24 hours, he cannot cultivate his fields properly. If it rained two days ago, it takes 10 hours to cultivate about a third of his fields. If it rained three days ago, he can cultivate about half of his fields in the same 10 hours. As each day without rain passes, he can work the ground proportionally faster. Thus, the ratio of field space prepared after 2 days compared to 3 days without rain is proportional to the ratio of field space prepared after 3 days compared to four days without rain. Express the portion of his field space that he can prepare in 10 hours if it has been 4 days since it rained. Write it as a simplified fraction in the box below.

| | of his field space

12. Which of the following descriptions would be a good way to think about multiplying 15 times 22?

Ⓐ Multiply 15 times 20, and add 2 more 20's.

Ⓑ Multiply 22 times 10, and then add half of that much again to your answer.

Ⓒ Break the 15 into 10 + 5 and the 22 into 20 + 2. Multiply the 10 times the 20 and the 5 times the 2. Add the two products together.

Ⓓ Round the 22 to 20. Think of the 20 as 2 times 10. Multiply the 15 times 2. Multiply your answer times 10. Add about 10 more to your answer since you rounded down earlier.

13. Which expression is equivalent to $\dfrac{a}{b}(2+c)$?

Ⓐ $\dfrac{2a}{b}+ac$

Ⓑ $\dfrac{1}{b}(2a+ac)$

Ⓒ $\dfrac{2a+c}{b}$

Ⓓ $\dfrac{2a}{bc}$

LumosLearning.com   ▶

14. Walter scored a 24 on his ACT. This was 80% of what his sister scored.

PART A

What was her score? Write your answer in the box below.

PART B

Explain how your determined your answer. Write your answer in the box below.

15. Use the number line to answer the question.

Which point might have a coordinate of $|t| + |w|$? Write your answer in the box below.

16. A famous author comes to terms with a publishing company and signs a contract for his newest book. The author will get $25,000 plus 15% of the proceeds of all book sales. The book sells for a price of $15.00. How many books will need to sell in order for the author to earn $47,500 in the first year? Write your answer in the box below.

_____ books need to sell.

17. At age 10, Micah weighed 88 pounds. According to the table, at what other age was his weight proportional? Write your answer in the box below.

Age	12	15	18	20	25
Weight	98	120	180	195	220

Years

18. A circle has a circumference of $16\pi k$ in. What is the ratio of the circumference of the circle to its area? Express the ratio in its simplest form and write it in the box below.

_____ : _____

19. A circle has an area of 49π ft². If you were to double the radius of the circle, what would the circumference of the new circle be in terms of π? Write your answer in the box below.

π ft

20. Cassidy's math teacher presents four situations to the class and wants to know which of them requires the use of the rational number $\dfrac{a}{b}$. Which situation is it?

Ⓐ Timothy needs to work fast enough to complete b problems in a hours. How many problems does he have to do each hour?

Ⓑ Timothy's class is going to be divided into a groups. There are b students in the class. How many students will be in each group?

Ⓒ Timothy has a dollars in his bank account. He wants to buy as many tickets to the game as he can. Each ticket costs b dollars. How many tickets can he buy?

Ⓓ Timothy wants to calculate his grade on the last test. There were a problems on the test. He got b problems right. What is the decimal form of his grade?

21. **Find the value of x. Write your answer in the box below.**

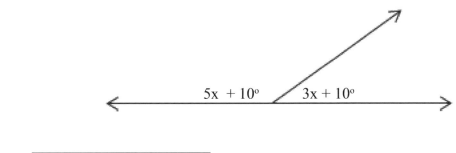

$5x + 10°$ $3x + 10°$

x =

22. Bradley has just started a new job 8 weeks ago. He is making plans for a vacation that he wants to take with his family. He wants to take 6 days off work for the vacation. His job allows him $\frac{1}{3}$ of a day's vacation time for each week that he works with the company. He has already taken 1 day of vacation time for some personal business he had to attend to. How many more weeks will Bradley need to work without taking vacation time before he has enough time built up to take his family on the vacation? Write your answer in the box below.

weeks

23. Ben and Blake both love to collect baseball cards. The ratio of cards that Ben has compared to the number that Blake has is 2:3. If Blake buys 500 more cards, he will have 3800 cards. How many cards does Ben currently own? Write your answer in the box below.

baseball cards.

24. It takes Craig 3 hours to drive to visit his parents. If he drives 20% faster, how long will it take him to drive that same distance? Express your answer in hours as a decimal and write it in the box below.

hours

25. A model airplane is built on a scale of 1:72 in comparison with the actual airplane. If one of the wheels on the model airplane has a radius of 0.25 in, what is the radius of the wheel of the actual airplane? Write your answer in the box below.

in

26. There are five siblings in Jennifer's family. The variability (range) of their ages is twice the mean of their ages. Which of the following sets of ages would fit this information?

Ⓐ | Ages | 10 | 18 | 15 | 8 | 3 |

Ⓑ | Ages | 21 | 5 | 7 | 9 | 3 |

Ⓒ | Ages | 10 | 12 | 15 | 13 | 2 |

Ⓓ | Ages | 42 | 46 | 29 | 33 | 38 |

27. Kyle is filling up a small ditch with gravel from his creek bed. He is carrying the gravel in a 5 gallon bucket. It takes him 2 minutes to walk from the creek to the ditch with a full bucket of gravel and only 1 minute to walk back with the empty bucket. It takes him 1 minute to fill the bucket with gravel. The ditch is approximately the shape of a half-cylinder with a radius of 1 ft and a length of 10 ft. A 5 gallon bucket is equivalent in volume to about 0.65 ft³. Kyle is just about to walk from the ditch to the creek for the first time with an empty bucket. It is 8:07 AM. What time will it be when he dumps the last bucket of gravel to fill up the ditch? Be sure to specify AM or PM when you write your answer in the box below.

Time:

28. Find the value of P that would make the statement true: 3P + 10Z = 2P (1.5 + 10Z)

Express your answer in decimal form in the box below.

P =

© Lumos Information Services 2014   LumosLearning.com   ▶

29. A survey was made of local citizens. The survey was designed to be representational of the general population by age categories. The table shows the number of citizens in each age category in the community. If the survey included 25 citizens from ages 20-29, how many must it have included from ages 40-49? Write your answer in the box below.

Age Category	10-19	20-29	30-39	40-49	50-59
Citizens	680	800	1310	1120	1050

Number of citizens from age 40-49 category.

30. Give the simplified value of the complex fraction in the box below: $\dfrac{\left(\dfrac{1}{3}\right)}{\left(\dfrac{\dfrac{2}{3}+2}{\dfrac{16}{3}}\right)}$

31. In a certain number game, you are asked to start with your age, A, double it, take away 4 years from it, divide it by 2, add 10 to it, double it again, take away 16, and finally divide it by 4. Which of the following expressions represents the final value in terms of A, your age?

Ⓐ $\dfrac{A}{2}$

Ⓑ $2A$

Ⓒ $A-10$

Ⓓ $2A+6$

Ⓔ A

32. Charley's boss promises him that if he works well for the next 3 months, he will get a 5% pay raise. If Charley currently earns d dollars per hour, which of the following is NOT a correct expression of what his new pay would be after the raise?

    Ⓐ   d +0.05

    Ⓑ   d(1+0.05)

    Ⓒ   1.05d

    Ⓓ   d + 0.05d

33. Kim bought a lawn chair that had a ticket price of $25.00. She ended up paying $26.50 after tax. If she were to buy a $40.00 patio table, how much would she have to pay after tax? Write your answer in the box below.

Price after tax: $ [   ]

End of End-Of-Year Assessment (EOY) - 2

     LumosLearning.com   ▶

End-Of-Year Assessment (EOY) - 2

Answer Key

Question No.	Answer	Related Lumos Online Workbook	CCSS
1	$\dfrac{9}{16}$	Solving Real World Problems	7.NS.3
2	D	Cross Sections of 3-D Figures	7.G.3
3	7.33 mph	Unit Rates	7.RP.1
4 Part A & B	C	Understanding Probability	7.SP.5
5	$\dfrac{1}{8}$	Finding the Probability of a Compound Event	7.SP.8a
6	8	Applying Ratios and Percents	7.RP.3-1
7	D	Rational Numbers, Addition & Subtraction	7.NS.1c-1
8	225 ft^2	Interpreting the Meanings of Expressions	7.EE.2
9	127	Solving Multi-Step Problems	7.EE.3
10	A	Rational Numbers, Addition & Subtraction	7.NS.1a
11	$\dfrac{3}{4}$	Applying Ratios and Percents	7.RP.3-1
12	B	Applying Properties to Rational Expressions	7.EE.1
13	B	Applying Properties to Rational Expressions	7.EE.1
14 Part A & B	30	Solving Real World Problems	7.NS.3
15	Point D	Rational Numbers, Addition & Subtraction	7.NS.1b-1
16	10,000	Solving Real World Problems	7.NS.3
17	Age 25	Understanding and Representing Proportions	7.RP.2a
18	1:4k	Circles	7.G.4-1
19	28π ft	Circles	7.G.4
20	C	Understanding and Representing Proportions	7.RP.2a
21	20°	Angles	7.G.5
22	13	Solving Real World Problems	7.NS.3
23	2200	Applying Ratios and Percents	7.RP.3
24	2.5	Understanding and Representing Proportions	7.RP.2c
25	18	Scale Models	7.G.1
26	B	Mean, Median, and Mean Absolute Deviation	7.SP.3

Question No.	Answer	Related Lumos Online Workbook	CCSS
27	9:47 AM	Solving Real World Problems	7.NS.3
28	0.5	Applying Properties to Rational Expressions	7.EE.1
29	35	Sampling a Population	7.SP.1
30	$\dfrac{2}{3}$	Rational Numbers, Multiplication & Division	7.NS.2b-1
31	$\dfrac{4}{2}$	Applying Properties to Rational Expressions	7.EE.1
32	A	Interpreting the Meanings of Expressions	7.EE.2
33	$42.40	Applying Ratios and Percents	7.RP.3-2

     LumosLearning.com   ▶

End-Of-Year Assessment (EOY) - 2

Detailed Explanations

Question No.	Answer	Detailed Explanation
1	$\dfrac{9}{16}$	Each piece of pizza is equivalent to $\dfrac{1}{8}$ of the pizza. Jeremy ate 3 pieces, so that is $\dfrac{3}{8}$ of the pizza. When Bill and Harley showed up, there were 3 pieces left, which would be $\dfrac{3}{8}$ of the pizza as well, but Bill only ate half of that. Half of $\dfrac{3}{8}$ is $\dfrac{3}{16}$. Add Jeremy's and Bill's amounts together: $\dfrac{3}{8} + \dfrac{3}{16} = \dfrac{9}{16}$ of the pizza.
2	D	If a circular drill bit passes through the center, it will leave a circular shape from top to bottom. This is exactly what the shape of a cylinder is.
3	7.33 mph	The first part of the ride took 75 minutes. The break was 10 minutes. That makes a total of 85 minutes. The whole time of his ride was 1 hour and 55 minutes, or 115 minutes. That means that the rest of the trip was 30 minutes, or 0.5 hours. The distance of the trip each way was $3\dfrac{2}{3}$ miles, so we divide the miles by the hours to get: $$3\dfrac{2}{3} \div 0.5 = 7.33 \text{ mph}$$
4 Part A & B	C	Because the probability is close to 1, it is likely. A probability of 1 would be a 100% chance of taking place. 0.93 is the same as a 93% chance of taking place.
5		Because half of the numbers on a six-sided die are even, the probability of rolling an even number one time is $\dfrac{1}{2}$. To compute the probability of doing this same thing three times in a row, we multiply the probability of each event together: $$\dfrac{1}{2} \times \dfrac{1}{2} \times \dfrac{1}{2} = \dfrac{1}{8}$$

Question No.	Answer	Detailed Explanation

6

Set up a proportion for the homeruns of each player:

$$\frac{3rd}{2nd} = \frac{1st}{ShortStop}$$

Fill in the shortstop's number of homeruns with the variable x, and we can express the 1st and 2nd basemen's amounts in terms of x:

$$\frac{3rd}{x+4} = \frac{2x}{x}$$

We know that the 3rd baseman also hit twice as many homeruns as the 2nd baseman, which means that his value must be 2(x + 4) = 2x + 8. How does this compare to the 2x of the 1st baseman? It is simply 8 homeruns more.

7

Because each week $3 is added to the total debt and $20 is subtracted from the debt, we could express the balance in this way:

150 + 3t – 20t.

Combining like terms, we have 150 – 17t.

8

What we want to do is to notice that 2x + 4 and 3x + 6, the values of the radius of each circle, can be compared. 3x + 6 is simply 2x + 4 multiplied by 1.5:

1.5 (2x + 4) = 3x + 6

So then, what happens to the area of a circle if the radius is 1.5 times as great? Using the formula for the area of a circle, replace r with 1.5r:

$A = \pi(1.5r)^2 = 2.25\pi r^2$

This is simply 2.25 times as great as the area was before the increase of the radius. Thus, the 100 ft^2 of the original circle is multiplied by 2.25, and we have 225 ft^2.

9

From the 100 head of mature cattle, we can expect there to be 60 calves. If 9 out of 10 survive, that gives us 54 that survive. If half of those are sold, that means that 27 of them remain to be added to the he2rd. This gives us, then, 127 head of cattle.

LumosLearning.com ▶

Question No.	Answer	Detailed Explanation
10		An additive inverse is simply the opposite value of a number such that when you add them together you have a sum of 0. Because Jan earns a positive amount in sales but her debt, a negative amount, is the same in value as the positive amount, the two values are opposites of one another. When we add these two amounts together, Jan has exactly 0 dollars.
11		Set up a proportion: $\dfrac{\frac{1}{3}}{\frac{1}{2}} = \dfrac{\frac{1}{2}}{x}$ Solve: $\dfrac{2x}{3} = \dfrac{1}{2}$ $4x = 3$ $x = \dfrac{3}{4}$
12		Multiply 22 times 10, and then add half of that much again to your answer. This works because 22 times 10 would be ten 22's, and half of that again would be another five 22's, which gives a total of fifteen 22's, which is what we need.
13		If we distribute only the a, we end up with: $\dfrac{1}{b}(2a + ac)$
14 Part A & B		Let s represent the sister's score. Set up an equation: $24 = (0.80)s$. Solve for s: $s = \dfrac{24}{0.80} = 30$
15		What we have to understand here is the nature of absolute values and how these work on a number line. The sum given to us is the sum of two different absolute values. Each one of these represents a positive value of the distance of each point from 0. Thus, however far t is from 0, that positive value gets added to the however far w is from 0. The result must be a total positive value that is farther from 0 than either t or w is. Thus, we need a point farther to the right than either t or w. Point D is the only such point on the number line.

Question No.	Answer	Detailed Explanation
16		Let n be the number of books sold, and set up an equation to solve: $47,500 = 25,000 + (0.15)(15)(n)$ $47,500 = 25,000 + 2.25n$ $22,500 = 2.25n$ $n = 10,000$
17		A ratio of 10:88 reduces to 5:44, or 1:8.8. The ratio at age 25 is 25:220, or 5:44, or 1:8.8, the same ratio.
18		Use the circumference formula to calculate the radius: $16\pi k = 2\pi r$ $r = 8k$ Use the radius to determine the area: $A = \pi(8k)^2 = 64\pi k^2$ Set up the ratio, and simplify: 16πk:64πk2 1:4k
19		Use the area to find the radius: $49\pi = \pi r^2$ $49 = r^2$ $r = 7$ Double the radius, and it is 14. Find the circumference: $C = 2\pi(14) = 28\pi$
20		Taking the total money available (a) and dividing by the cost of each ticket (b) will get you the number of tickets that can be purchased: $\frac{a}{b}$
21		Because these two angles form a straight line, they must have a total degree measure of 180 degrees when added together. Set up an equation to this effect, and solve for x: $5x + 10 + 3x + 10 = 180$ $8x + 20 = 180$ $8x = 160$ $x = 20$

Question No.	Answer	Detailed Explanation
22		After 8 weeks of work, he has accumulated $\frac{8}{3}$ days of vacation time, but he has spent one full day, which means he now has only $\frac{5}{3}$ days available. Set up an equation that shows a starting value of $\frac{5}{3}$ and adds $\frac{1}{3}$ for each week, t, and is equal to the needed 6 days. Solve for t: $$\frac{5}{3}+\frac{1}{3}t=6$$ $$\frac{1}{3}t=6-\frac{5}{3}$$ $$\frac{1}{3}t=\frac{13}{3}$$ $$t=13$$
23		Subtracting the hypothetical 500 additional cards that Blake might buy, we find that he currently has 3300 cards. If the ratio of Ben's to Blake's cards is 2:3, we know that Ben has $\frac{2}{3}$ as many cards as Blake, which would amount to 2200 cards.
24		Use the formula D = RT. Solving for T, we have $T=\frac{D}{R}$ Replace the R with 1.2R to represent the 20% increase in speed. The distance remains the same. How will the time vary?: $$T=\frac{D}{1.2R}=\left(\frac{5}{6}\right)\left(\frac{D}{R}\right)$$ We see that the time is $\frac{5}{6}$ of what it was, which would amount to a total of 2.5 hours.
25		Simply multiply the model airplane's radius by 72 to obtain the full scale radius: (0.25)(72) = 18 inches.
26		The range of the data for answer B is 21 − 3 = 18 years. The average of the ages is: $$\frac{21+5+7+9+3}{5}=\frac{45}{5}=9$$,which means that the range is twice the mean.

Question No.	Answer	Detailed Explanation
27		Let's start by calculating how much total volume of gravel is needed to fill the ditch. The volume is half that of a cylinder with a radius of 1 ft and a length of 10 ft:

$$A = (0.5)(10)(\pi)(1)^2 = 5\pi\, ft^3 \approx 15.71\, ft^3$$

Now let's calculate how many buckets are needed: $\dfrac{15.71}{0.65} = 24.17$

buckets

This means that he will have to carry 25 buckets to fill the ditch completely. Each trip takes him a total of 4 minutes, so this means he needs to carry gravel for 100 minutes altogether. Starting at 8:07 AM, he will be done at 9:47 AM.

28

Distribute on the right side and compare:

$$3P + 10Z = 2P(1.5 + 10Z)$$

$$3P + 10Z = 3p + 20PZ$$

You can see that the only way this expression will be the same on both sides is if 10 is the same as 20P. This means P must be 0.5.

29

Set up a proportion using the numbers from the survey and the numbers from the population:

$$\frac{x}{25} = \frac{1120}{800}$$

$$x = 35$$

30

Simplify using the order of operations:

$$\frac{\left(\dfrac{1}{3}\right)}{\left(\dfrac{\dfrac{2}{3}+2}{\dfrac{16}{3}}\right)} = \frac{\left(\dfrac{1}{3}\right)}{\left(\dfrac{\dfrac{8}{3}}{\dfrac{16}{3}}\right)} = \frac{\left(\dfrac{1}{3}\right)}{\left(\dfrac{1}{2}\right)} = \frac{2}{3}$$

31

Follow the process step by step, starting with A:

A

2A

2A − 4

A − 2

A + 8

2A + 16

2A

$$\frac{A}{2}$$

Question No.	Answer	Detailed Explanation
32	A	A is an incorrect expression because it simply takes Charley's current pay rate and adds five cents to it rather than adding 5% of the rate.
33		Set up a proportion using both pre-tax prices and both after-tax prices: $$\frac{26.50}{25} = \frac{x}{40}$$ $$x = 42.40$$

Notes

 LumosLearning.com

Notes

Lumos StepUp™ is an educational App that helps students learn and master grade-level skills in Math and English Language Arts.

The list of features includes:

- Learn Anywhere, Anytime!

- Grades 3-8 Mathematics and English Language Arts

- Get instant access to the Common Core State Standards

- One full-length sample practice test in all Grades and Subjects

- Full-length Practice Tests, Partial Tests and Standards-based Tests

- 2 Test Modes: Normal mode and Learning mode

- Learning Mode gives the user a step-by-step explanation if the answer is wrong

- Access to Online Workbooks

- Provides ability to directly scan QR Codes

- And it's completely FREE!

http://lumoslearning.com/a/stepup-app

About Online Workbooks

• When you buy this book, 1 year access to online workbooks included

• Access them anytime from a computer with an internet connection

• Adheres to the New Common Core State Standards

• Includes progress reports

• Instant feedback and self-paced

• Ability to review incorrect answers

• Parents and Teachers can assist in student's learning by reviewing their areas of difficulty

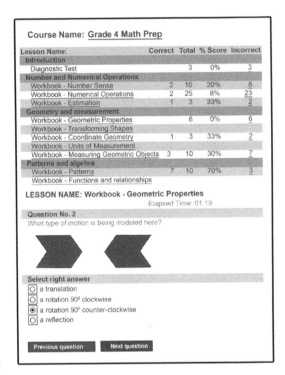

Course Name: Grade 4 Math Prep				
Lesson Name:	Correct	Total	% Score	Incorrect
Introduction				
Diagnostic Test		3	0%	3
Number and Numerical Operations				
Workbook - Number Sense	2	10	20%	8
Workbook - Numerical Operations	2	25	8%	23
Workbook - Estimation	1	3	33%	2
Geometry and measurement				
Workbook - Geometric Properties		6	0%	6
Workbook - Transforming Shapes				
Workbook - Coordinate Geometry	1	3	33%	2
Workbook - Units of Measurement				
Workbook - Measuring Geometric Objects	3	10	30%	7
Patterns and algebra				
Workbook - Patterns	7	10	70%	3
Workbook - Functions and relationships				

LESSON NAME: Workbook - Geometric Properties
Elapsed Time: 01:19

Question No. 2
What type of motion is being modeled here?

Select right answer
- ◯ a translation
- ◯ a rotation 90° clockwise
- ◉ a rotation 90° counter-clockwise
- ◯ a reflection

[Previous question] [Next question]

Report Name: Missed Questions

Student Name: Lisa Colbright
Cours Name: Grade 4 Math Prep
Lesson Name: Diagnostic Test

The faces on a number cube are labeled with the numbers 1 through 6. What is the probability of rolling a number greater than 4?

Answer Explanation

(C) On a standard number cube, there are six possible outcomes. Of those outcomes, 2 of them are greater than 4. Thus, the probability of rolling a number greater than 4 is "2 out of 6" or 2/6.

A)		1/6
B)		1/3
C)	Correct Answer	2/6
D)		3/6

Made in the USA
Lexington, KY
08 November 2014

Once upon a time there lived a farmer who had three sons. The older lads, Petro and Havrilo, were clever fellows. But their younger brother, Ivan, was small and simple. He spent his days playing with a leather ball. Even so, he was always cheerful and kind, which more than made up for his lack of wit. Of all his sons, the farmer loved Ivan best.

One day the farmer summoned his sons. "It is time to decide who will inherit the farm. It is also time for you boys to be married. Go now—ride out into the world. Whoever brings back the most beautiful wedding kerchief will be my heir."

Petro and Havrilo set out at once. But Ivan stayed home, sitting on the fence, tossing his ball from hand to hand.

"Ivan?" his father asked. "Why aren't you looking for a kerchief?"

"Don't be angry, Father," Ivan pleaded. "My brothers can have the farm. I only want to play with my ball."

"Don't give up, Ivan," his father insisted. "Try your best. Who knows?
You might be lucky."

Ivan agreed to try. He hitched their old mare to a rickety wagon and
rolled off down the road.

The road wound through a marsh. Water covered the path. But the
old mare kept plodding along as if she knew where she was going.

After a while they came to a castle. At the gate the guards
saluted. "We've been expecting you, Lord Ivan!" they meowed.
For they were all cats dressed in colorful uniforms.

Ivan stared at the sight. I suppose there's nothing to fear,
they're only cats, he thought as he drove through the gate.

"Welcome! Welcome!" Throngs of cats greeted him. They were all dressed as lords and ladies, with powdered wigs and high-heeled shoes. They led Ivan into a ballroom, where a cat orchestra played lively music.

"Ivan, what has kept you so long?" A green-eyed cat took his hand.

She must be their queen, Ivan thought. "I'm sorry I was delayed," he replied.

"Did you bring us a present?"

Ivan took the leather ball from his pocket. "I . . . I brought you this."

"A *ball*!" shrieked the cats. "Throw it! *Throw it!*"

Ivan tossed the ball. It bounced across the room. The cats chased it down hallways and stairs, never stopping until their wigs came off and all their fine clothes were in tatters.

"What joy you have given us!" cried the cat queen. She handed Ivan a walnut.

"Don't open it until you get home. You will find something nice inside."

Ivan said farewell. He climbed into his wagon and returned the way he had come.

He found his brothers waiting for him, flaunting the beautiful wedding kerchiefs they had found on their travels. "What did you find, Ivan?" his father asked.

"I'm not sure," Ivan said. He cracked the walnut. Inside lay a shining silk kerchief embroidered with gold thread. It made his brothers' kerchiefs look like nose rags.

"Ivan has won," his father said. "The farm will be his."

"You can't leave the farm to a simpleton!" his brothers protested.

"I don't want my brothers to quarrel," Ivan told his father. "They can have the farm. I'll be happy to sit on the fence, whistling. . . ."

"We will try another test," the farmer said. "Go out into the world and bring back the most beautiful wedding dresses you can find. The farm will belong to whoever returns with the most beautiful wedding dress."

Petro and Havrilo set out at once. Ivan remained sitting on the fence beside the mint patch, whistling to himself.

"Won't you even try?" his father pleaded. "You were lucky last time. You might be lucky again."

"If you insist, Father. I will do the best I can."

Ivan stuffed his pockets with mint leaves. Then he set out again. Straight as an arrow, the mare made her way to the castle of the cats.

"Welcome back, Lord Ivan!" the cats cried.

"What have you brought us this time?" the cat queen asked.

"Something you will like." Ivan reached into his pockets. He threw handfuls of mint leaves into the air.

"*Catnip!*" shrieked the cats. They flung themselves on the leaves, leaping and rolling until their clothes came unbuttoned and their wigs went askew.

"Ivan, you are wonderful beyond words to bring us catnip! I must give you something in return." The cat queen handed him an acorn. "Remember, don't open it until you reach home."

Ivan arrived to find his brothers showing off the wedding dresses they had found on their travels. "What did you bring back, Ivan?" their father asked.

"I'm not sure," Ivan replied. He cracked the acorn. Out fell the most exquisite wedding dress, so beautiful that it made the others look like dishrags. Petro and Havrilo stamped their feet. "We don't care how beautiful that dress is! You can't leave the farm to a simpleton!"

"Let my brothers have the farm," Ivan said. "I'll be happy to whittle sticks. That is all I want."

"Nonsense!" said his father. "We will try one more test. If Ivan wins again it will prove that fortune favors him. Go now. Seek brides for yourselves. Whoever returns with the most beautiful bride will inherit the farm."

Petro and Havrilo set forth at once. Ivan stayed back, whittling a stick.

"Aren't you even going to try?" his father asked.

"How can I find a bride, Father? Maidens don't fit in walnuts or acorns."

"You have been lucky before. Maybe you'll be lucky again."

Sighing, Ivan climbed into the wagon and set out. He let the mare go where she liked. Sure enough, she took him straight to the castle of the cats.

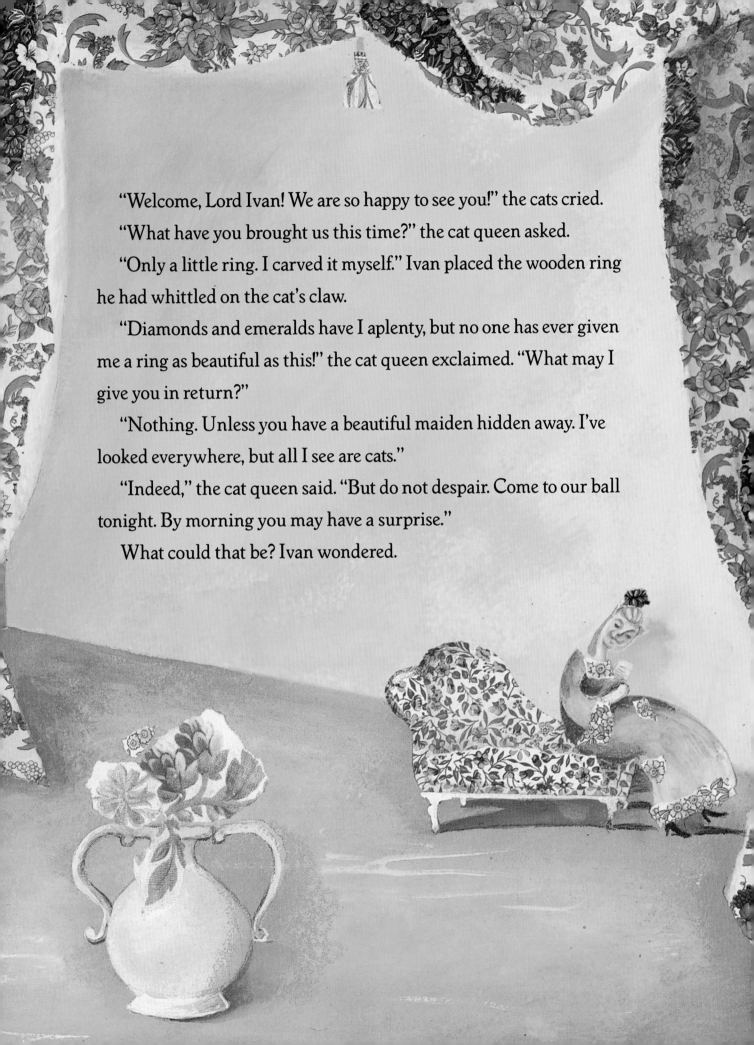

"Welcome, Lord Ivan! We are so happy to see you!" the cats cried.

"What have you brought us this time?" the cat queen asked.

"Only a little ring. I carved it myself." Ivan placed the wooden ring he had whittled on the cat's claw.

"Diamonds and emeralds have I aplenty, but no one has ever given me a ring as beautiful as this!" the cat queen exclaimed. "What may I give you in return?"

"Nothing. Unless you have a beautiful maiden hidden away. I've looked everywhere, but all I see are cats."

"Indeed," the cat queen said. "But do not despair. Come to our ball tonight. By morning you may have a surprise."

What could that be? Ivan wondered.

Ivan danced the night away in the castle of the cats. Suddenly all the clocks began striking midnight. The cats hurried away, leaving Ivan alone in the ballroom.

He wandered around the castle, looking for the cats, but he found not a whisker. So he tucked himself into a great gilded bed and went to sleep.

"Ivan, wake up!"

Ivan opened his eyes. Sunlight streamed through the window. At the foot of his bed stood the most beautiful woman he had ever seen.

"Who are you?" Ivan gasped.

"Why, Ivan! Don't you recognize your betrothed bride?" She showed him the carved wooden ring on her finger. At once Ivan understood that she was the cat queen herself.

"Hurry! Get dressed. We must away."

The cat queen led Ivan to the courtyard. A golden coach pulled by eight splendid steeds stood on the spot where he had left his mare and old wagon. The coach was attended by footmen and grooms dressed in shining livery. They all had almond-shaped eyes and extremely long whiskers.

Away they all galloped, until the coach arrived at Ivan's home.
He found the house decorated for a wedding. Petro and Havrilo had brought back two beautiful brides. The maidens were extremely lovely. But when Ivan's bride stepped from the coach, they covered their faces.

"Ivan has won again. His bride is the most beautiful of all," the farmer declared.

"The farm is his," Petro and Havrilo at last agreed.

"No," said Ivan. "You keep the farm. I don't need it. I have everything I want."

The three brothers were married that day. After the wedding Ivan
and his bride got in their coach and drove off, never to be seen again.

Except every now and then a traveler appears, telling a strange tale
of spending the night in a mysterious castle inhabited by cats. Their
queen is a beautiful snow white cat, and their king, an elegant tom
who tosses a leather ball from paw to paw.

Now what do you make of that?

AUTHOR'S NOTE

The Castle of the Cats is based on "The Palace of the Cats," a Latvian folktale. Since both Katya
Krenina and I have deep personal ties to Ukraine, we felt more comfortable setting the story
there. As Katya put it, "I can do Latvia, but my heart is in Ukraine."

To Katya
E. A. K.

To the memory of my mother,
the angel who lives in my heart always
K. K.

Text copyright © 2004 by Eric A. Kimmel · Illustrations copyright © 2004 by Katya Krenina · All Rights Reserved ·
Printed in the United States of America · www.holidayhouse.com · First Edition · 1 3 5 7 9 10 8 6 4 2
Library of Congress Cataloging-in-Publication Data · Kimmel, Eric A. · The castle of the cats / retold by Eric A. Kimmel;
illustrated by Katya Krenina.—1st ed. · p. cm. · ISBN 0-8234-1565-1 (hardcover) · [1. Fairy tales. 2. Folklore—Ukraine.]
I. Krenina, Katya, ill. II. Title. · PZ8+ · 398.2'09477—dc21 · 2001024776